UNDERSTANDING BREXIT

Why Britain Voted to Leave the European Union

SOCIETYNOW SERIES

SocietyNow: short, informed books, explaining why our world is the way it is, now.

The *SocietyNow* series provides readers with a definitive snapshot of the events, phenomena and issues that are defining our 21st century world. Written by leading experts in their fields, and publishing as each subject is being contemplated across the globe, titles in the series offer a thoughtful, concise and rapid response to the major political and economic events and social and cultural trends of our time.

SocietyNow makes the best of academic expertise accessible to a wider audience, to help readers untangle the complexities of each topic and make sense of our world the way it is, now.

Titles in this series

UNDERSTANDING BREXIT

Why Britain Voted to Leave the European Union

By

GRAHAM TAYLOR
University of the West of England, UK

United Kingdom — North America — Japan
India — Malaysia — China

Emerald Publishing Limited
Howard House, Wagon Lane, Bingley BD16 1WA, UK

First edition 2017

British Library Cataloguing in Publication Data
A catalogue record for this book is available from the British
Library

ISBN: 978-1-78714-679-2 (Print)
ISBN: 978-1-78714-678-5 (Online)
ISBN: 978-1-78743-006-8 (Epub)

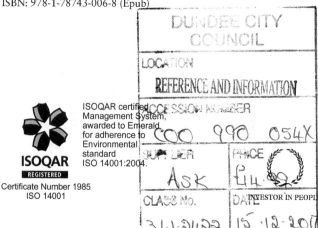

CONTENTS

ACKNOWLEDGEMENTS

During the writing of this book, I have benefitted from discussions about Brexit and related issues with students and colleagues from UWE, Bristol including Steve Hunt, Andy Mathers, Miles Thompson, Ian Walmsley and Gunter Walzenbach. I am also grateful to Hilary Taylor for her support during the writing and preparation of this text.

LIST OF ABBREVIATIONS

AES	Alternative Economic Strategy
AIFMD	Alternative Investment Fund Managers Directive
ASLEF	Associated Society of Locomotive Engineers and Firemen
BAME	Black, Asian and Minority Ethnic
BNP	British National Party
ECSC	European Coal and Steel Community
ECU	European Currency Unit
EDL	English Defence League
EEC	European Economic Community
EFSM	European Financial Stabilization Mechanism
EMS	European Monetary System
EMU	Economic and Monetary Union
ERM	Exchange Rate Mechanism
EU	European Union
FDI	Foreign Direct Investment
GDP	Gross Domestic Product
NATO	North Atlantic Treaty Organization
QMV	Qualified Majority Voting
SDP	Social Democratic Party
SGP	Stability and Growth Pact

SNP	Scottish National Party
TTIP	Trans-Atlantic Trade and Investment Partnership
UKIP	United Kingdom Independence Party
WTO	World Trade Organization

CHAPTER ONE

INTRODUCTION: 'BREXIT MEANS BREXIT!' OR DOES IT?

On 23 June 2016, the British people voted narrowly to leave the European Union (EU). In the toxic political aftermath of the Brexit referendum, many Leave supporters were already expressing paranoid fears that the will of 'the people' to leave the EU would be subverted by liberal elites and Brussels bureaucrats. The newly elected prime minister, and Remain supporter, Theresa May, tried to calm their concerns with the now infamous phrase: 'Brexit means Brexit'. While this phrase has become widely parodied as a robotic and meaningless tautology (which, of course, it is), it does serve to highlight a common-sense view that the meaning of Brexit does not extend beyond the political and legal relationship between the United Kingdom (UK) and the EU. The main purpose of this book is to question this simple assumption and to demonstrate how this narrow definition of Brexit does not exhaust its possible meanings and significance. Questions about the sovereignty of the United Kingdom were undoubtedly important during the referendum, and the question of national sovereignty provided the master frame for the Leave campaign — reflected in the campaign mantras of 'I want my country back' and 'take back control'. There is also the possibility, however, that the issue of sovereignty was a proxy for a range of economic, cultural and political concerns and insecurities that extended far beyond the constitutional and legal status of the relationship between the United Kingdom and the EU. The issues of immigration, political disengagement and economic insecurity were particularly important concerns that found expression in the referendum, and these were successfully harnessed and articulated by the Leave campaigns.

During the past decade, there has been a rapid growth in immigration to the United Kingdom, particularly immigration from EU member states in Central and Eastern Europe. Immigration was a central issue in the EU referendum, and public anger and insecurity around this issue was systematically exploited by the Leave campaigns. The issue of immigration signalled concerns about the pressure that the large-scale and unplanned influx of EU workers was placing on labour markets, housing and public services. It also expressed deeper cultural insecurities and fears connected to how immigration, alongside broader processes of imperial decline, globalization, European integration and UK devolution, was impacting negatively on British culture and the meaning and significance of 'Britishness'. This was linked to a longstanding process of political disengagement amongst many segments of the British electorate, which was illustrated by declining turnout during elections, declining support and membership of the main political parties and an increasing distrust and disillusionment with political elites and 'expert opinion'. Political elites became widely perceived as remote and unrepresentative and associated with 'progressive' and 'politically correct' opinions and values that had become disconnected from the opinions and values of 'ordinary' people. Concerns over immigration, British identity and political elites dovetailed with a range of grievances, anxieties and insecurities connected to the restructuring of the British economy. The global importance of the City of London as a financial hub highlights the importance of the financial sector to the British economy and successive governments have privileged the sector over industrial and manufacturing sectors. The 'financialization' of the British economy resulted in the de-industrialization of many areas that were formerly dominated by industries such as mining, steel-making and shipbuilding and this produced devastating long-term problems such as declining employment opportunities and decaying communities. During the past two decades, the reform of the professions and public services have generalized insecurity amongst intermediate and middle-class segments of society, and many lower-level service sector jobs have become increasingly precarious and linked to insecure working practices such as zero-hours contracts and enforced self-employment. The 2008 financial crisis, and the subsequent austerity programmes, exacerbated the negative effects of these economic trends and developments, and the resulting grievances and anxieties were captured and articulated by expressions of radical right political populism resulting ultimately in Brexit. Paradoxically, this conservative reaction against globalization was mobilized, orchestrated and financed by a fragment of the political and economic elite with libertarian and hyperglobalist values and interests. While these developments only coalesced into a visible populist force during the past decade, the underlying dynamics and contradictions have been decades in the making.

The central argument of this book is that the roots of Brexit can be traced back over many decades, and that such an historical analysis is vital if we are to understand *how* and *why* Brexit happened. The decision to leave the EU is the most visible tip of an iceberg of long-term social, political and economic change. Hidden beneath the surface of this iceberg is a matrix of economic, socio-cultural and political dynamics that have wrought fundamental changes to the British state and British society, and the relationship between the United Kingdom, Europe and the rest of the world. Brexit was the point at which four long-term trajectories of British development converged and precipitated an event of seismic magnitude that disrupted decades of what seemed like inevitable transnational integration and development. First, the post-imperial crisis of the British state fuelled a discourse of British exceptionalism and a range of contested interpretations of 'Britain', 'Britishness' and 'Europe' that attempted to maintain this 'exceptionalism' in the context of post-imperial decline. This resulted in the United Kingdom being peripheral to the process of European integration and fuelled ambivalent and negative public attitudes towards European integration. Second, the 'financialization' of the British economy created a tension between the global and European integration of the British economy and a pattern of de-industrialization and economic insecurity that undermined the legitimacy of elites and elite projects such as the EU. Third, the secular decline in the strength and coherence of British culture and identity and a trajectory of cultural decline resulting from immigration, loss of empire, the devolution of the United Kingdom and the transnational dynamics of globalization and European integration. This encouraged the emergence of new popular nationalisms and sub-nationalisms and increasingly politicized and Eurosceptical forms of English identity. Fourth, the de-alignment of party political representation in Britain and the increasing convergence of mainstream parties around an agenda of economic and social liberalism. This created a crisis of legitimacy amongst the marginal and insecure that could be harnessed and exploited by Eurosceptic movements and parties of the populist right. These dynamics were interrelated and mutually reinforcing and culminated ultimately in the 'perfect storm' of Brexit.

Brexit has long historical roots and its consequences are likely to stretch decades into the future. Two decades ago, the ideology of 'Third Way' social democracy (Giddens, 1994, 1998), combined with an established academic (Albrow, 1996; Beck, 2000; Giddens, 1990) and business (Friedman, 2000; Ohmae, 1995) orthodoxy, to stress the inevitability, irreversibility and desirability of globalization. This made European integration and the division of the world into regional trading blocs one of the defining and ineluctable characteristics of the age (Castells, 2000b; Giddens, 2006; Urry, 2003). The idea that Britain could or should leave the EU was firmly relegated to the arcane world of right-wing think tanks and policy geeks. The speed at which this idea has not only entered the political mainstream, but been presented to the British people as an in-out referendum, highlights the intensity of the dynamics underpinning Brexit. Lanchester (2016) has argued that Brexit illustrates the operation of an 'Overton window' (see Beck, 2010) that defines the acceptable range of political thought in a culture at a given moment and which is subject to movement. The idea of Britain exiting the EU moved in a relatively short time-frame from right-wing think-tankery to journalistic fellow travellers, to the fringe of electoral politics and then, after hardening into serious possibility, to the political mainstream. Brexit will perhaps emerge as the moment when neo-liberalism and globalization reached the limits of their contradictory development. Brexit has challenged the enduring myth that neo-liberalism and globalization are the inevitable and inexorable facts of contemporary life. The populist movement that led to Brexit challenged key elements of globalization such as immigration, transnational regulation and the dominance of technocratic experts. It articulated a demand to re-establish national economic governance, which included controls on immigration, the introduction of tariffs on international trade, state aid for industry and national industrial strategies. Brexit provides empirical proof that globalization was never inevitable, and confirms the well-founded arguments of sceptics who highlighted consistently how transnational constructions were social constructions and always contingent (Hardy & McCann, 2017; Martell, 2007; Ray, 2007). This could ultimately be a difficult lesson for the hyper-globalist elites that orchestrated Brexit to learn: Brexit unleashing a populist anti-globalization force and demands for national control that will prove inimical to its own long-term interests.

In retrospect, it is perhaps not so surprising that Brexit happened, and that it happened in a nation known as 'reluctant Europeans' and an 'awkward partner' in the EU (Hobolt, 2016). The quotidian reality of the EU, and the specificity of the UK's relationship with the EU, should perhaps have been good indications that a Brexit was not only possible, but perhaps inevitable. The EU exhibits many of the flaws attributed to it by its Eurosceptical critics. The logic of European integration was always intended to insulate the regulation of European markets from democratic scrutiny and control, and the 'democratic deficit' is fundamental to the organizational logic of the EU (Carchedi, 2001; Milward, 2000; Streeck, 2014, 2015). This was evident from the origins of European integration with the post-war development of coal and iron markets in the European Coal and Steel Community (ECSC) to its broader manifestation as the common market and customs union following the formation of the European Economic Community (EEC) in 1957. This included a broad competition and trade policy and a single market in agriculture and fisheries regulated by the Common Agricultural Policy (CAP) and the Common Fisheries Policy. In the late 1980s, the *Single European Act* (SEA) established the single market resting on the 'four freedoms' of goods, people, capital and services. In the 1980s, neo-liberalism was embedded into the institutions and practices of the EU (Bieler, 2006, pp. 9–12; Van Apeldoorn, 2001). This began with the European Monetary System (EMS) in 1979, which aligned member state economies with the German economy through the Exchange Rate Mechanism (ERM) to prevent currency depreciation and to maintain low inflation. The Maastricht Treaty or *Treaty on European Union* (TEU) of 1992 resulted in Economic and Monetary Union (EMU) and the introduction of the single currency in 1999. This vested control of monetary policy in a politically-unaccountable European Central Bank (ECB) and the 'convergence criteria' leading to EMU, reinforced by the 1997 *Stability and Growth Pact*, imposed cuts in public expenditure and borrowing, and limits to budget deficits and government debt. In 2000, the Lisbon Summit launched a new method of 'open coordination' to sustain economic growth, through the setting of benchmarks to encourage economic competitiveness, liberalized financial markets and a knowledge-based economy. Following the 2008 economic crisis, the 2012 *Treaty on Stability, Coordination and Governance in the Economic and Monetary Union* produced an institutional framework for the regulation of Eurozone economies through which the European Commission can issue sanctions against nation states with 'excessive' deficits or macro-economic imbalances. While these mechanisms of neo-liberal rationalization are, to some extent, balanced by 'social cohesion' measures, such as the 'Social Chapter', the undemocratic and technocratic tendencies of the EU are clearly more than a figment of the Eurosceptical imagination.

The British public has been consistently the most Eurosceptic member state in the EU since joining in 1973. Despite this history of wariness and often outright hostility to European integration, the United Kingdom has been remarkably successful in shaping the policies and institutional trajectory of the EU. In 1988, Margaret Thatcher made a speech to the *College of Europe* in Bruges, which attacked the incipient federalism of the EU. While this is often seen as a defining moment in the deepening of Euroscepticism in the United Kingdom, the substantive agenda set out by Thatcher in this speech became the accepted principles of European integration: namely, intergovernmentalism; enterprise and the eradication of barriers to trade; and the strengthening European security under the umbrella of North Atlantic Treaty Organization (NATO). In addition, UK political leaders secured 'opt outs' in respect to the Euro, the *Schengen Accord* on free movement and aspects of the Charter of Fundamental Rights. The success of the United Kingdom in Europe was achieved in a context of deepening Euroscepticism. In contrast to other EU member states, leading members of a governing political party, the Conservative Party, were vehemently anti-EU and this allowed Euroscepticism into the political mainstream (De Vries & Edwards, 2009). Despite being an 'awkward partner', the United Kingdom managed to carve out a privileged position for itself within the EU (Menon & Salter, 2016, p. 1301) that, nevertheless, remained mainly unrecognized and unappreciated by an ambivalent British public. The tension between relative effectiveness and relative hostility helps to explain the absence of a long-term or systematic attempt to convince the British people of the benefits of EU membership (Menon & Salter, 2016, p. 1298) and illustrates further why Brexit should not be considered such a surprise after all. There should also have been warning signs from previous EU referenda. Despite the confidence of the Remain side that elite support could deliver victory in the referendum, the examples of previous EU referenda in Denmark and Ireland showed that referenda generate highly unpredictable results and that voters often reject the recommendations of mainstream parties and experts (Franklin, Marsh, & McLaren, 1994, 1995; Hobolt, 2009). Indeed, Brexit is part of a European-wide phenomenon where populist parties have achieved electoral success pursuing an agenda based on concerns about immigration, lack of economic opportunities and disenchantment with the political class (Hobolt & Tilley, 2016; Kriesi et al., 2012). These developments provide an important context for understanding the development and strength of Euroscepticism in the United Kingdom, but to properly understand Brexit we need to dig deeper and wider.

UNDERSTANDING BREXIT

In recent years, Euroscepticism has increased across EU member states. Populist parties and movements have emerged across Europe and exit from the EU is often central to their political programmes (Hooghe & Marks, 2007; Taggart, 1998; Usherwood & Startin, 2013; Vasilopoulou, 2013). There is a body of established research on the origins and form of opposition to European integration. This research has usefully differentiated between 'hard' and 'soft' Euroscepticism, and has attempted to locate the origins of Euroscepticism at the intersection between ideology and the organization of party political systems. This can provide useful comparative insights into how Euroscepticism varies in intensity and form across time and space, and why it has been particularly virulent in the United Kingdom. However, it provides only limited insights into *why* the United Kingdom has so far been the only member state to not only consider leaving the EU, but to actually initiate the exit procedure. It fails to adequately address the political economy of Brexit or the relationship between Brexit, culture and identity. It is only by examining the politics of Brexit in this broader analytical framework that we can adequately address the question as to why a Brexit was always more likely than a Frexit in France, a Grexit in Greece or a Nexit in the Netherlands. The main chapters of this book explore the geo-political, economic, socio-cultural and political developments and dynamics that will provide a deeper understanding of *why* Brexit happened and *why* and *how* it happened *now*.

In Chapter Two, I explore the geo-political and economic dynamics associated with Brexit. I begin with an exploration of the geo-political roots of Brexit, with a focus on how the attempt to maintain the status of the United Kingdom as a 'world power' in the context of post-imperial decline defined the peripheral relationship of the United Kingdom to European integration. In the context of this decline, a range of Eurosceptical political discourses emerged on the right and left of British politics that attempted to redefine the meaning of 'Britain', 'Britishness' and 'Europe' in ways that confirmed and re-affirmed this 'exceptionalism'. These discourses framed the accession of the United Kingdom to the EEC and continued to frame the relationship between the United Kingdom and the EU throughout the following four decades. This is followed by an exploration of how the uneasy relationship between the United Kingdom and 'Europe' has also been defined by a structural mismatch between the developmental trajectories of the British and Continental economies. I highlight how the development of a dynamic form of financialized 'Anglo-capitalism' resulted in London becoming a dynamic growth hub in the global financial system, and the ways in which this created an increasing tension between the European and global integration of the British economy. This financialized trajectory was also responsible for the de-industrialization of the British economy and increasing levels of economic and social inequality and insecurity in the post-industrial heartlands. This consistently threatened the legitimacy of the British state and resulted in the 'state projects' of Thatcherism and New Labour, which attempted to encourage the dynamism of the UK's financialized economy, while building the active consent to this ongoing accumulation amongst strategically important sectors of British society. I demonstrate how both the 'organic' patriotism of Thatcherism and the universal cosmopolitanism of New Labour contributed to the accretion of Eurosceptical attitudes within British society and to the building of significant middle-class and working-class support bases for the radical right programme of populism that would culminate with Brexit. The 2008 financial crisis intensified inequality and marginalization in the United Kingdom and, in the context of high levels of EU immigration, Eurosceptical attitudes intensified and provided the context for a form of radical right populism that would develop into the support base for the UK Independence Party (UKIP), the Leave campaign and ultimately Brexit. The chapter concludes with a discussion of how this tension between 'market fundamentalism' and a radical right reaction is anticipated in the work of Karl Polanyi (1944, 2001), and how this was reflected in the tensions between the 'libertarian' and 'conservative' segments of the Brexit coalition.

In Chapter Three, I explore the socio-cultural dynamics underpinning Brexit through a critical evaluation of the 'two tribes' thesis that has dominated popular discourse and debates on Brexit. This thesis suggests that the two sides in the referendum campaign represented opposing cultures marked by dominant and subaltern identities: Remain-supporting 'winners', marked by the cultural values of cosmopolitan liberalism and multiculturalism, and Leave-supporting 'losers', marked by the values of communitarianism, nativism and patriotism. The chapter highlights how this discourse can undermine an effective analysis of the socio-cultural dynamics of Brexit. The 'scapegoating' of marginal groups such as the 'white working class', who are often presented as too 'stupid' and 'prejudiced' to recognize their own 'real' economic interests, ignores or downplays the real anger and alienation that underpinned support for Leave in marginal communities. This focus also downplays the importance of middle-class supporters of Brexit who, in terms of absolute number of votes cast, were more significant than working-class supporters of Brexit. The chapter critically evaluates the category of the 'left behind' Brexit supporter, and highlights how the concept is useful only if it is broadened from a narrow socio-economic category to a cultural disposition across sections of the working class, intermediate class and middle class. Within this broader framework, the 'left behind' can be linked to the 'class trajectory' of individuals across the class structure in situations where personal social decline is linked to wider class decline and expressed as a form of 'resentful nationalism' (Fenton, 2012; Mann & Fenton, 2009). The chapter concludes with an exploration of the 'culture wars' that developed around the issue of immigration before and during the referendum campaign, and the ways in which class, race and nation were combined in forms of toxic 'resentful nationalism' to deliver support for Brexit.

In Chapter Four, I explore the political and electoral dynamics underpinning Brexit. The chapter highlights the divisions and corrosive effects of the 'Europe question' in British politics throughout the post-war period. The attempt by the 1997–2010 New Labour governments to depoliticize this question and to develop a technocratic approach to European integration fanned the flames of an insurgent radical right populism that harnessed concerns and grievances over EU immigration and the post-2008 austerity programmes and pinned the blame squarely at the door of the remote and undemocratic EU. The chapter demonstrates how the development of New Labour was part of a broader process of political realignment that resulted in political parties becoming increasingly disconnected from their political support base and subject to declining democratic legitimacy. In the context of the declining support for the mainstream political parties and increasing turbulence in patterns of political support and alignment, popular grievances and concerns found expression in forms of Eurosceptic populism that were successfully harnessed and articulated by UKIP and the Eurosceptic right in the Conservative Party. This is followed by an exploration of the socio-economic and socio-cultural composition of the coalition that developed to express this populism, both within and beyond UKIP, and how this coalesced into an effective campaigning force in the EU referendum. The chapter concludes with an assessment of how the elite-led and funded Leave coalition was able to effectively mobilize public support through a populist repertoire of contention focused on how the EU was a corrupt and undemocratic institution that protected the interests of rich and powerful elites, and how leaving the EU would enable 'the people' to 'take back control' of Britain's economic and political destiny and protect the British way of life through the strengthening of borders and controls on immigration.

In the concluding chapter, I explore the economic, cultural and political trajectories of post-Brexit developments in Britain. The main economic trajectory has been a deepening crisis of free market neo-liberal capitalism, which is reflected in the rhetoric and policy proposal of both the Conservative Party and the Labour Party. However, this rhetorical embrace of 'organized capitalism' is not reflected in the negotiating position of the British government in the Brexit negotiations, and this has the potential to aggravate further the grievances and anxieties that underpinned support for Brexit. The populist forces associated with Brexit assaulted the longstanding liberal consensus from the right, and the chapter proceeds to explore how this defines the key socio-cultural trajectory of Brexit towards increasing levels of ethnic, racial and inter-cultural tension and hatred. In the face of insults, threats and intimidation, many EU migrants have left or are planning to leave the United Kingdom. The chapter then explores the main political trajectory following Brexit, which has been towards the de-alignment of the main political parties on the basis of a range of issues and concerns raised by Brexit. The resulting tensions have generated political paralysis in the ruling Conservative Party, and an unstable and ambiguous coalition within the Labour Party, between the Corbynite leadership and membership base, the 'New Labour' parliamentary Party and the party's working-class and predominantly pro-Brexit support base. The chapter concludes by assessing the importance of Brexit as part of a global trajectory of anti-elite, nationalistic populism that has developed across the world following the 2008 financial crisis.

CHAPTER TWO

RELUCTANT EUROPEANS? AN ECONOMIC HISTORY OF EUROPEAN INTEGRATION IN THE UNITED KINGDOM

The British are often described as 'reluctant Europeans' or the 'awkward partner' of the EU. This reflects the dominant self-image of the British as 'exceptional' and 'separate' from Continental Europe. The legacy of Empire played an important role in the development of this self-image. Britain had been an imperial power, with an Empire stretching to the four corners of the world, and had bestowed to this imperial realm all the hallmarks of British exceptionalism: economic liberalism, parliamentary democracy and the English language. Europe was viewed through the prism of this exceptionalism, as a place of imperial rivals, threatening ideologies and cultural difference. The notions of 'separation' and 'exceptionalism' have continued to shape the geo-political relationship between the United Kingdom, Europe and the rest of the world, despite the declining imperial status of the United Kingdom. The idea that the United Kingdom has an independent destiny separate from the Continent has been an important driver of ideological Euroscepticism. This has fused with the distinctive pattern of economic development in the United Kingdom to amplify the peripheral status of Britain to broader patterns of European development and integration. While the United Kingdom was a 'reluctant European', sitting somewhat uncomfortably at the table of European integration, it was simultaneously pursuing a global role as a financial superpower and establishing the City of London as a principal hub in the global financial system. The tension between the global and European integration of the British economy has generated tensions and contradictions between the United Kingdom and other EU member states, and provided the context for a series of struggles over the meaning of 'Britain', 'Britishness' and 'Europe' which have been fought out within the declining post-imperial British state. I will begin with an exploration of these geo-political and economic dynamics, as they set the parameters of the broad structural context within which the process of understanding Brexit can begin.

THE LONG SHADOW OF EMPIRE: EUROPEAN INTEGRATION AND THE GEO-POLITICS OF POST-IMPERIAL DECLINE

The legacy of Empire has cast a long shadow over the geo-political relationship between the United Kingdom and 'Europe'. The attempt to maintain the status of the United Kingdom as a 'world power' with exceptional interests and priorities has defined the peripheral and semi-detached status of the United Kingdom to the process of European integration, and the uneasy relationship between the United Kingdom and European institutions. This uneasy relationship between the United Kingdom and 'Europe' has a long history and predates the UK's membership of the EEC. In 1945, the UK economy was bankrupt, but British elites were concerned with maintaining the position of the United Kingdom as a 'world power'. This status was defined by the UK's position at the centre of the Empire/Commonwealth and by the UK's 'special relationship' with the United States. The United Kingdom played a central role in 'Cold War' politics between 1945 and 1955; including the establishment of NATO, the development of an independent nuclear deterrent and a key role in the reconstruction and integration of Europe through the US-funded Marshall Aid programme (Deighton, 1993). The latter included the ECSC, which integrated the French and West German economies through the pooling of sovereignty in steel and coal resources. While the United Kingdom played an important role in the foundation of the ECSC, it refused to join and, when this developed into the EEC following the Treaty of Rome in 1957, Britain was invited to join, but again refused. The assumption, at that time, was that the Second World War did not require a radical re-thinking of Britain's relationship with Europe. This was articulated by Winston Churchill in 1947, when he stated that Britain was a 'world power', which occupied a unique position as one of three interlocking circles — Empire, the Unites States and 'Europe' (Forster, 2002, p. 11). European integration was rejected as it would have undermined the assumptions of 'greatness' that underpinned the self-belief of British elites.

During the late 1950s, the scale of Britain's economic and diplomatic decline became increasingly evident. This was reflected in the diplomatic and military humiliation of the United Kingdom in the Suez Crisis, and the comparatively poor performance of the British economy. While there was enduring political opposition to EEC membership across the political spectrum, the economic case for joining the EEC became increasingly compelling, and the Conservative Government, led by Harold Macmillan, decided to apply for membership of the EEC (Kaiser, 1993). This was a logical concomitant of the 'cooperative multinationalism' that had marked UK foreign policy since 1945 (Freedman, 2016), and a pragmatic acceptance of the 'economic' case for European integration. The United Kingdom applied to join the EEC in 1963 and 1967, but both applications were vetoed by the French President, Charles de Gaulle, because the economic interests of the United Kingdom and Europe were considered incompatible owing to the close relationship between the United Kingdom and the United States. Following de Gaulle's departure from office, and his replacement by Georges Pompidou, Edward Heath secured Britain's entry to the EEC in 1973. This marked an attempt to manage post-imperial decline through European integration. The process of accession was, however, highly contested, and the resulting struggles over the meaning of 'Europe', and its relationship to the crisis of the post-imperial British state, determined both the terms of the debate over accession (Nairn, 1973), and the turbulent relationship between the United Kingdom and Europe for the next four decades. The meaning of 'Britain' and 'Britishness' and the idea of British exceptionalism became key ideological elements in the struggle over the meaning of 'Europe'.

The period leading to UK accession to the EEC was marked by political turbulence, economic decline and industrial unrest; including the start of the 'troubles' in Northern Ireland and the intense industrial unrest over the ill-fated 1971 *Industrial Relations Act*. The main impetus to accession was economic. Membership of the EEC was opposed by powerful financial interests in the City, but in 1971, this was reversed when a global financial crisis followed a decision by the United States to suspend the convertibility of the dollar to gold (Clarke, 1988, pp. 342–344). Representatives of industrial capital were already supportive of EEC membership; seduced by expanding investment opportunities, corporatist coordination and cooperative industrial relations. This enabled Conservative Prime Minister, Edward Heath, to unite business interests and Conservative grassroots activists behind a pro-EEC Conservative Party strategy (Nairn, 1973, pp. 9–33). The main opponents to EEC entry came from the nativist right and the Labourite and Marxist left, who, in different ways, elevated 'nation' over party and class. On the left, Tony Benn and his supporters rejected the narrow protectionism of the EEC and appealed to a broader internationalism embracing the Commonwealth and beyond. The EEC was against the 'national interest' because it prevented the development of an independent socialist Britain and inhibited the expression of a radical and popular *British* labourism — a sublimated nationalism constructed through the universalist discourse of 'social imperialism' (Nairn, 1973, pp. 67–73). On the right, a marginalized Enoch Powell opposed membership because it would destroy British sovereignty and prevent a revival of English nationhood (Forster, 2002, p. 39). The legacy of Powell would later re-emerge to define the forms of Euroscepticism associated with Thatcherism. The strong 'organic' patriotism inherited from Powell, along with the market fundamentalism of Milton Friedman and Friedrich von Hayek, defined the geo-politics of Thatcherism: a commitment to global free trade and the liberalization of international markets, alongside an opposition to supranational institutions and the federalism of European integration. This brand of ideological Euroscepticism was also to re-emerge as the bedrock of UKIP policies and programme in the period leading to the EU referendum (Seymour, 2015, p. 36).

The accession of the United Kingdom to the EEC did not resolve the 'Europe question', but set the scene for four decades of awkward and uneasy relations between the United Kingdom and its European partners. When the Conservatives re-entered government in 1979, Margaret Thatcher demanded that Britain's budgetary settlement be re-negotiated and, in 1984, following years of belligerent rhetoric and bad-tempered bargaining, managed to secure a rebate on Britain's contribution to the EEC. In 1988, Thatcher made her now infamous Bruges speech in which she rejected European federalism and the growth of supranational institutions in favour of a Europe based on cooperation between sovereign nation states. The Maastricht crisis of the Major government was a key moment in the growth and consolidation of Euroscepticism in the Conservative Party. When John Major replaced Margaret Thatcher in 1990, he signalled his intention to establish a less confrontational relationship with the EU, which included membership of the ERM: an arrangement introduced in 1979, as part of the EMS, which was designed to reduce exchange rate variation and achieve monetary stability in preparation for EMU. In the initial development of the single currency, a model of EMU based on a City-inspired, market-based 'hard' European Currency Unit (ECU) was proposed by the United Kingdom, but this was rejected in favour of a German model of EMU, based on a Bundesbank-inspired, institutionally regulated Euro-currency (Dyson, 2000, p. 903). The latter was perceived as a threat to the financial pre-eminence and competitive advantages of the City, and this was reflected in declining political support for the ERM within the Conservative Party. The resulting loss of confidence, along with an over-valued pound and high interest rates in Germany, led to the events of 'Black Wednesday' in September 1992, when sterling was forced to withdraw from the ERM.

The events surrounding 'Black Wednesday' highlighted the tension between European integration and the position of the United Kingdom in global financial markets. This fuelled a growing Eurosceptic discourse that highlighted the flawed nature of the EMU project. In the Maastricht negotiations, the United Kingdom secured opt-outs on monetary union and the Social Chapter. Despite these concessions, and the discursive packaging of the Maastricht Treaty as a Thatcherite, free market version of European integration, Major was unable to ward off a successful rebellion in the Maastricht ratification debate in Parliament. The most significant aspect of this rebellion was the call for a referendum to enable 'the people' to decide the fate of the Maastricht Treaty. The opposition to Maastricht highlighted the emergence of a right-wing popular movement against European integration, which was supported by important sections of the media. This development secured the hegemony of the Thatcherite approach to the EU within the Conservative Party (Gifford, 2006, p. 858) and resulted in a range of new Eurosceptic foundations, movements and political parties that opposed European integration on the grounds of British exceptionalism and sovereignty. These included the European Foundation, the Referendum Party and the Anti-Federalist League.

The post-Maastricht problem for UK governments became how to maintain British influence within the EU, while avoiding the potentially negative implications of being drawn into the institutional arrangements of European integration (Gifford, 2016, p. 785). The election of New Labour in 1997 resulted in a change of emphasis and presentation in UK relations with the EU. The New Labour project included the 'Europeanization' of policy and strategy, including an embrace of European institutions and initiatives, such as the single market, the Social Chapter and the ERM (Holden, 1999; Ladrech, 1994). However, despite the Europhile rhetoric, there were important continuities with the established resistance to further European integration, and the United

Kingdom continued to engage with EMU from a position of national autonomy and superiority (Gifford, 2016, p. 788). The official position of the 1997–2010 New Labour administrations to EMU was 'prepare and decide'; underpinned by Gordon Brown's five economic tests. However, rather than aligning the United Kingdom with the Eurozone, New Labour prioritized the need for structural reform in other EU member states. New Labour attempted to resolve the tensions and contradictions between the global and European integration of the British economy through the alignment of other EU national economies with the financialized interests of the United Kingdom. In 2000, the *Lisbon Summit* endorsed a Europeanized version of New Labour's 'Third Way'. This based the reform of the European Social Model on the New Labour principles of economic competitiveness, liberalized financial markets and a knowledge-based economy. This policy initiative was underpinned by a belief that globalization had transformed the logic of European integration: the logic of internal integration and harmonization was replaced by the logic of a UK model of flexibility, fairness and macroeconomic stability within nation state economies. The interests of the City and the potential benefits arising from the de-regulation of European financial markets were central to this new political economy (Lee, 2009, p. 24). The Euro was launched in 1999 and, by the following year, the City was handling more international Euro-dominated transactions than Paris and Frankfurt combined (Kynaston, 2002, p. 785).

The belief that Britain was a 'world power' with an 'exceptional' history and developmental trajectory defined by the legacy of Empire and the financial pre-eminence of the City, continued to define the relationship between the United Kingdom and 'Europe' throughout the eras of Thatcherism and New Labour. In different ways, both these projects were attempts to redefine and reinvigorate the meaning and significance of 'Britishness' in the context of post-imperial decline. Both emerged as movements within their respective parties with a mission to demolish the obstacles to British greatness and prosperity, and both attempted to reconnect 'state' and 'nation' in an era defined by globalization and demands for devolution within the United Kingdom (Nairn, 2001, p. 9). Thatcherism undermined the class basis of the traditionalist British state through a radical economic programme of liberalization that attacked corporatism and familial advantage, but propped up and worshipped the idea of the British state through invocations of monarchy and timeless union. The result was a populist Euroscepticism, defined by opposition to political interdependence, and a commitment to laissez-faire in the global economy, and minimal but strong government on a domestic level (Baker, Gamble, & Ludlam, 1993). The populist appeal of this position rested on how a conservative and regressive ideology could simultaneously appear contemporary and radical (Gifford, 2006, p. 857).

New Labour continued the neo-liberal trajectory of the Thatcher era, but combined this with radical plans for the modernization of the British state and a more generalized battle against, what Tony Blair described as, 'the forces of conservativism'. However, the devolution programme, and the aborted plans for the reform of the House of Lords, together with the 'corporate populism' of 'Ukania plc', could not conceal the ultimate conservativism of the New Labour project. New Labour articulated a 'corporate nationalism', that dressed the defence of the British constitutional state in the clothes of 'Cool Britannia', and attempted to combine an appeal to 'Middle England' with a commitment to multicultural cosmopolitanism and 'Europe'. The botched constitutional reform of the British state left the 'England question' unresolved and encouraged the development of an increasingly toxic form of English nationalism (Nairn, 2005). While the Thatcherite and New Labour discursive constructions of 'Britain' and 'Europe' were diametrically opposed, both contributed to forms of ideological Euroscepticism that would find expression in the forms of anti-EU populism that resulted ultimately in Brexit. Euroscepticism emerged as the principal guardian of a set of powerful national myths concerning the sovereignty of British parliament and British exceptionalism (Wallace, 1991). Britain's former imperial greatness has, therefore, continued to cast a long shadow since the UK accession to the EEC in 1973. The resulting tensions and contradictions have also been shaped, and further reinforced, by the distinctive economic model of 'Anglo-capitalism' in the United Kingdom.

ANGLO-CAPITALISM AND THE ECONOMICS OF BREXIT

The uneasy relationship between the United Kingdom and the EU has also been defined by a structural mismatch between the developmental trajectories of the British and Continental economies. This has generated a tension between the global and European integration of the British economy that has shaped and been shaped by the geo-political relationship between the United Kingdom and 'Europe' outlined above. This mismatch has been generated by the financialization of the British economy and the importance of London as a hub in the global financial system. The role of the City of London as a global financial hub provided the impetus for the United Kingdom to play a leading role in the construction of the EU single market, but also explains the resistance of the United Kingdom to further European integration. In order to understand the relationship between Brexit, neo-liberalism and European integration, it is important not to reduce the EU to a transnational agent of neo-liberalism (Bonefeld, 2002; Bonefeld & Burnham, 1998; Gill, 1998; Van Apeldoorn, 2002), or an arena in which national modes of regulated capitalism are articulated and compete (Garrett, 1998; Hall & Soskice, 2001; Hay, 2004; Hirst & Thompson, 2000; Parker, 2008; Strange, 2006). The EU is most usefully understood as a form of 'open regionalism' (Baker, Gamble, & Seawright, 2002), through which the relationship between EU member states and neo-liberal globalism is mediated. The distinctive, finance-led model of British capitalism has a more direct relationship to neo-liberal globalism compared to other EU economies, and neo-liberal globalism has tended, therefore, to mediate the relationship between the United Kingdom and the EU (Gifford, 2016, p. 783).

The post-war development of the British economy was marked by a flawed state-led industrialization strategy, which was marked by low levels of growth, productivity and competitiveness, and a crisis-ridden trajectory that undermined the fiscal base, steering capacity and legitimacy of the British state (Clarke, 1988). The model of 'Fordist' industrialization that developed in the United Kingdom was seriously flawed, and the attempt to resolve the resulting crisis through monetarism and financialization generated a distinctive 'Anglo-model' of capitalist growth and development. In other advanced European economies, the post-war period was marked by an extended period of 'Fordist' growth. This growth model comprised a 'regime of accumulation', based on mass production, high productivity and wage growth, which was balanced and held in place by a 'mode of regulation', based on Keynesian state corporatism and social democratic assumptions of full employment and universal welfare (Aglietta, 1979; Harvey, 1989; Lipietz, 1987). In the United Kingdom, the British state lacked the *dirigiste* capacity to engage in statist intervention or corporatist coordination, but failed to pursue a consistent laissez-faire strategy owing to the paternalism of traditional 'One Nation' conservatism and the strength and opposition of the labour movement. The UK economy failed to match the high levels of growth and productivity achieved in Continental Europe and Scandinavia, but became embedded in the financial circuits of Atlantic Fordism and the world economy. The entry of the United Kingdom into the EEC in 1973 was an attempt to resolve the crisis through an alignment and integration of the UK economy with high-growth and high-productivity corporatist economies in Western Europe. Following the oil shock of 1973, national Fordist settlements came under severe strain and started to be displaced by post-Fordist flexibility and innovation and monetarist economics. The post-Fordist trajectory of the United Kingdom reflected the flawed industrialization strategy of the Fordist era and resulted in an accumulation strategy based on de-industrialization and financialization, rather than the post-Fordist innovation and knowledge-led growth, developed in Germany and other Continental economies (Jessop, 2017, p. 135). There has, therefore, been an enduring non-alignment between the United Kingdom and Continental economies since 1945.

The distinctive 'Anglo-model' of capitalism emerged as the combined product of path-dependent global economic change, the agency of political elites and government strategies (Gifford, 2016, p. 784). The Anglo-model predated the election of the Thatcher government in 1979, but Thatcherism played a vital role in dismantling the institutional obstacles of post-war Keynesianism and state planning that would allow and encourage the City of London to assume a hegemonic position in the global financial system. In the early 1970s, the Treasury and the Bank of England made a series of regulatory changes that elevated the interests of financial markets over those of industry. The new framework made the price mechanism the principal criterion in the allocation of credit (Needham, 2014), and reforms included a relaxation of exchange and credit controls, the reduction of stamp duty on share and bond transactions, the abolition of dividend payment controls and cuts in corporation tax. The Labour Government led by James Callaghan adopted a monetarist economic strategy in response to the oil crisis, and following the intervention of the International Monetary Fund in 1976, the UK economy was integrated into the neo-liberal Washington Consensus and the management of the international accumulation crisis through a process of 'accelerating financialization' (Panitch, 2000). In 1979, the Thatcher administration removed capital controls and, in 1986, 'Big Bang' de-regulation opened the City to foreign banks and securities companies. The City developed a highly-internationalized banking sector (Hirst & Thompson, 2000, pp. 347–348), and became established as the financial gateway to Europe, and a leading offshore destination for the profits of US multinationals attempting to escape tax and regulation. The City developed as the key site of transnational integration in Europe and became responsible for the management of billions of Euros for the EU public and private sectors.

From the mid-1970s, the British economy was transformed from an industrial economy, with substantial manufacturing and extractive sectors, to a post-industrial service economy, dominated by the financial sector. Between 1979 and 1989, investment in financial services increased by 320.3%, compared to a 12.8% increase in manufacturing. Between 1970 and 2010, manufacturing declined from 30% of GDP to 13% of GDP; manufacturing employment fell from 35% to 10% of total UK employment; and there was a shift from a trade surplus of between 4% and 6% and a trade deficit of between 2% and 4% (Chang, 2010; Coates, 1995;

Davis & Walsh, 2015). Financialization became the dominant strategy of successive governments from 1975 onwards, and this had three important consequences on British society (Jessop, 2017, pp. 135–136). First, the interests of financial capital dominated those of industrial capital, subaltern classes and marginal communities. Second, an unsustainable debt-fuelled boom developed based on fictitious credit and this generated a visible polarization of wealth and income. Third, neo-liberal policies reinforced the de-industrialization of the British economy and remaining industries were left vulnerable to foreign takeover. In this context, the British economy became dominated by a low-skill, low-tech, low-wage service sector and increasingly insecure and precarious forms of employment. This was combined with the effects of a liberal approach to EU immigration following the accession of nation states from Central and Eastern Europe, which put further pressure on labour markets and public services. This neo-liberal strategy also underpinned public investment decisions that intensified the uneven regional development to the benefit of London and the South East of England.

These problems were seriously intensified by the 2008 global financial crisis. The 2008 crisis was generated by the transnational integration of credit relations and the contagion effect of the collapse of the US sub-prime mortgage market. This resulted in a 'credit crunch' as financial institutions had 'leveraged' or borrowed against toxic asset-backed securities that had become worthless (Foster & Magdoff, 2009). This combined with the domestic dynamics of the 'Big Bang' de-regulation of the City and an asset-backed expansion of credit (Kirkland, 2015). The state bailouts of banks and financial institutions following the crisis increased government debt and resulted in a programme of austerity to reduce this debt. The UK economy was re-stabilized through the nationalization and recapitalization of the banking sector and a programme of 'quantitative easing' by the Bank of England. In the context of this economic restructuring, British governments were forced to deal with two interrelated problems: how to maintain legitimacy in the context of increasing levels of inequality and how to manage and reconcile the financialized trajectory of the UK economy with European integration. The political 'state projects' of Thatcherism and New Labour were attempts to maintain the legitimacy of the British state alongside an increasingly global and financialized 'accumulation strategy' and the ongoing project of European integration. The initial success of these projects was, however, short-lived and both were to contribute to the growing Eurosceptical discourse that was to culminate in Brexit.

BREXIT AND THE 'ORGANIC' CRISIS OF THE BRITISH STATE

The financialization of the British economy has resulted in a pattern of uneven development between London and the South East and the former industrial heartlands, alongside increasing levels of inequality, insecurity and marginalization and an increasingly visible polarization of wealth and incomes. This has contributed towards a long-term or 'organic' crisis of legitimacy within the British state, and a series of hegemonic projects have developed to overcome this crisis of legitimacy. The ways in which these projects have unfolded has contributed to the accretion of Euroscepticism at various levels of the social structure and determined the balance of forces that supported Brexit in the 2016 referendum. In the referendum, the British people defied the leadership and advice of political and economic elites and voted to leave the EU. In this context, it is possible to understand Brexit as a 'conjunctural' episode in an ongoing 'organic' crisis of 'hegemony' that can be traced back to the mid-1960s (Jessop, 2017, p. 134). The Italian political theorist, Antonio Gramsci, differentiated between such short-term or 'conjunctural' crises and long-term or 'organic' crises of hegemony. The latter can last for decades and require the re-shaping of state institutions and the development of new ideologies to re-establish hegemony or the active consent of society to capitalist accumulation (see Simon, 1982). Thatcherism and New Labour were 'passive revolutions' within this ongoing crisis. Gramsci defined a 'passive revolution' as a major transformation within the capitalist mode of production, whereby the relations of production and domination are modified to overcome obstacles to further accumulation. These revolutions are politically conservative-adaptive, led by reactionary forces and involve both coercion and ideological consent. While both Thatcherism and New Labour were initially progressive in removing obstacles for further accumulation and accentuating the dynamism of the financialized trajectory of the British economy, both unleashed forces of reaction and conservativism that contributed towards an incipient Eurosceptic populism.

The 'state project' of Thatcherism played a key role in the development of both the Anglo-model of economic development and the intensification of ideological Euroscepticism. Thatcherism mobilized key sections of the working and middle-class into a 'productivist alliance' that challenged social democratic obstacles to free market liberalism, through a contradictory and unstable project of 'authoritarian populism'. This project was a flexible blend of 'authoritarian' neo-conservativism and 'libertarian' neo-liberalism (Hall, 1983; Hay, 1996; Jessop, Bonnett, Bromley, & Ling, 1988, pp. 127–140). While the former focused on the reassertion of traditional moral values, dismantling the dependency culture of the welfare state and elevating the importance of patriotism, the latter focused on the liberalization of markets and encouraging private enterprise, entrepreneurial attitudes and property ownership. Thatcherism was supported by a 'two nations' legitimation strategy, which rewarded the enterprising, hardworking and home-owning 'haves', while disciplining the inefficient and deviant 'have nots', within an ideological framework of organic patriotic nationalism inherited from the Powellism of the 1970s. This ideological framework fused economic individualism with an organic patriotism, and this resulted in increasingly individualized forms of Euroscepticism amongst the 'haves' of the two nations project. As we will see in chapter four, older, middle-class, Conservative-supporting voters from the South of England were one of the main constituents of the Leave vote in the 2016 referendum. Thatcherism eventually imploded as the 'minimal state' strategy failed to maintain the conditions for successful accumulation and was subject to declining legitimacy amongst the 'haves' in its 'Middle England' support base (Hay, 1996, pp. 170−172).

The 'passive revolution' of New Labour was an attempt to address the 'Schumpeterian deficit' (Hay, 1996, pp. 172−173) of the Thatcherite state, through an accumulation strategy that continued the emphasis on economic globalization and financialization, but with a social interventionist state strategy that attempted to encourage innovation and competitiveness in order to construct a 'growth niche' within the global economy. This resulted in a focus on macro-economic stability to maintain the confidence of financial markets, supply-side employability reforms, low levels of personal and corporate taxation, flexible labour markets and an 'enabling' industrial policy (Glyn & Wood, 2001). The 'Third Way' approach of New Labour combined a commitment to neo-liberal financialization and marketization, alongside the adoption of a post-Keynesian endogenous growth theory premised on the notion that supply-side reforms of markets and welfare could achieve both economic efficiency and social justice and fairness (Buckler & Dolowitz, 2004). New Labour developed a 'one nation' legitimation strategy that attempted to appeal to both those parts of the 'Middle England' constituency it had inherited from Thatcherism and its traditional working-class support base. This involved the construction of a new globalized 'citizen-consumer' subject. This subject was as an active agent and 'stakeholder' with the state and the market, and supported the values of 'social progress', multiculturalism and liberal cosmopolitanism, while passively accepting the inevitability of neo-liberal capitalism (Steinberg & Johnson, 2004, pp. 31–32). The problem of social inequality was transformed into the problem of social exclusion from the market, which was tackled through the 'positive welfare' policies on child poverty, social exclusion and the expansion of state employment (Lavery, 2017, pp. 5–6). This legitimation strategy could not endure the 2008 financial crisis, but it had already started to unravel before the crisis owing to the ways in which the technocratic forms of governance developed by New Labour de-linked the party from its traditional working-class support base and undermined its democratic legitimacy (Mair, 2000). As mentioned earlier, New Labour's botched attempt to modernize the British state had intensified English nationalism, and as immigration from the EU increased and the impact of the 2008 crisis started to bite, another key component in the Brexit support base started to emerge: the English working-class Eurosceptics made politically homeless by the technocratic neo-liberalism and progressive cosmopolitanism of New Labour.

The 'passive revolutions' of Thatcherism and New Labour contributed the two main constituencies of support for Brexit: the nativist and Thatcherite middle class and the former-Labour supporting English working class. The legitimation strategy of the 2010–2015 Conservative-led coalition government intensified the Euroscepticism within both these constituencies. The Coalition government developed a 'two nations' legitimation strategy that continued the finance-led neo-liberal accumulation strategy, alongside, austerity, welfare cuts and a squeeze on wage-levels. Between the crisis and 2015, there was a 10.4% reduction in the level of real wages in the United Kingdom, compared with an increase in real wages of 23% in Germany and an OECD average increase of 6.7% (TUC, 2016c). In 2015, 20% of jobs in the United Kingdom paid less than the voluntary living wage (TUC, 2015). There was a growth of non-standard forms of employment such as zero-hours contracts, part-time working and involuntary self-employment in labour markets that were already blighted by low levels of pay. These developments were compounded by cuts in public spending, including cuts to working tax credits, housing and disability benefits that fell disproportionately on marginalized individuals and communities. The 'two nations' legitimation strategy was underpinned by a discourse that distinguished between the deserving and undeserving poor in terms of 'strivers' and 'skivers', and this encouraged a 'moralized' antagonism between different groups in society (Lavery, 2017, pp. 8–10). This scapegoating and labelling of marginalized groups provided the perfect conditions for the development of a powerful 'resentful nationalism' (Fenton, 2012; Mann & Fenton, 2009; Seymour, 2015, p. 35) based on claims for national entitlement and priority. Immigration continued to increase under the Coalition government, and in the context of declining wages and welfare retrenchment, working-class English nationalism developed an increasingly Eurosceptic flavour. This was compounded by the ways in which leading members of the Coalition started to link the Eurozone crisis with the failed recovery of the British economy, and the increasingly virulent Eurosceptic rhetoric that was developed by leading Conservative politicians and within the right-wing media to frame relations between the United Kingdom and the EU. These Eurosceptical currents started to articulate a 'logic of exit', while further de-legitimating the elites that supported and were associated with the EU.

THE EUROZONE CRISIS AND THE LOGIC OF EXIT

While Brexit has deep roots, it is unlikely to have occurred in the absence of the 2008 financial crisis and its skewed class-based recovery. The 2008 crisis deepened the 'organic crisis' of hegemony within British state and society. In the context of ongoing fiscal and financial crises and persistently high levels of inequality and social polarization, the possibility of hegemony was undermined by long-running divisions in the Establishment; a marked cleavage amongst business and financial elites; and the declining popularity of the mainstream political parties (Jessop, 2017, p. 134). The global economic crisis of 2008 and the onset of the Eurozone crisis resulted in a further shift in the British narrative on EMU: from reform to failure and the argument that the Eurozone posed an obstacle to British recovery from the crisis. In response to the Eurozone crisis, the EU generalized the austerity measures that had been imposed on Greece and Ireland through the 'Fiscal Compact' associated with the *Treaty on Stability, Coordination and Governance in the EMU* of 2012. Within this framework, the Stability and Growth Pact targets of Eurozone economies are policed by the Commission and the European Court of Justice; marking the further embedding of neo-liberalism within the institutions of the EU, and the development of what Streeck (2014, 2015) has termed the 'European consolidation state'. The 2008 crisis, and the subsequent Fiscal Compact, strengthened the role of Germany within the EU, and was widely perceived in the United Kingdom as a threat to the 'special relationship' between the United Kingdom and the United States and the interests of the City. The level of political and economic Euroscepticism increased markedly during the 2010–2015 Coalition government led by David Cameron.

The governing elite in the United Kingdom started to further distance itself from the crisis in the Eurozone, through a narrative that stressed the need to protect the national interest from the threats posed by further European integration. At the 2011 European Council, the United Kingdom resisted and opposed the extension of EU-level financial supervision and the harmonization of financial and fiscal regulation. As we will see in chapter four, this reflected the concerns of Party supporters and financial donors from the City about the regulation of the financial sector by the EU. The United Kingdom refused to contribute to the *European Financial Stabilization Mechanism* (EFSM), rejected the idea of an EU banking union and challenged the use of 'Qualified Majority Voting' (QMV) on matters of financial supervision. The resulting Treaty went ahead without the inclusion of the United Kingdom, and the United Kingdom was excluded from future negotiations. This overt expression of national sovereignty allowed Cameron and the Coalition Chancellor, George Osborne, to blame the Eurozone for the UK's continuing recession. This intensified the discourse that the Eurozone was a failure and a threat to British economic recovery and made 'exit' a legitimate political and economic position (Gifford, 2016, pp. 789–790). In a range of political interventions, leading Eurosceptics started to articulate the logic of a Brexit in a way that stressed the global openness of the United Kingdom compared with the Eurozone, and highlighted the potential for bilateral trade deals with major global players such as China, India, Australia, Russia and

Brazil. This was made easier because of the ways in which growing inequality in the United Kingdom was linked to the Eurozone crisis (Watkins, 2016, p. 9). After 2010, sterling became a haven for capital fleeing the Euro debt crisis, and the resulting London-centred growth provided employment opportunities for migrants escaping recession-hit Euroland. The proportion of the workforce born outside the United Kingdom was 10% in 2015 and these workers were disproportionately employed in the lowest quintile of the labour market in direct competition with the most marginalized and precarious British-born workers (Eurofound, 2016; ONS, 2015).

David Cameron attempted to address the resulting Euroscepticism with the promise of a 'new deal' for the United Kingdom in Europe followed by an in-out referendum. Cameron embraced the popular turn of Euroscepticism: the threat of Eurozone integration could now only be addressed through an appeal to 'sovereignty' and 'the people' (Gifford, 2014). In his 2013 Bloomberg speech, David Cameron set out a vision of a reconstituted relationship between the United Kingdom and the EU based on a vision of a 'flexible union of free member states'. The new Europe would be principally concerned with further liberalization and globalization of the single market. In negotiating a 'new deal' for the United Kingdom within the EU, Cameron attempted to bypass the core EU value of the indivisibility of the 'four freedoms', but was dependent on EU institutions and member states for the success of this strategy. This produced an awkward compromise that provided for an emergency brake on benefits for EU migrants, while leaving the fundamental principle of free movement within the EU intact. This new deal was condemned as a sham by Eurosceptics and vilified in the right-wing press. An elite compromise could not withstand the force of a popular nationalist agenda driven by

Euroscepticism (Gifford, 2016, p. 791). The supporters of Brexit could present a case that combined notions of indivisible sovereignty with a progressive economic strategy based on the United Kingdom as an open and global trading nation outside a declining and crisis-ridden Eurozone.

The imperial legacy of the United Kingdom helps to explain why the mantra of 'take back control' associated with the decision to Brexit should have such a particular resonance in the United Kingdom. In the context of the Brexit referendum in the United Kingdom, it resonated with a perceived loss of control over economics, politics and identity and permeated deep within the national psyche (Bachmann & Sidaway, 2016). The geo-political decline of a formerly hegemonic nation, intertwined with waves of post-war immigration from former colonies, also set the context for the racist undercurrent of the debate on Brexit and immigration (Tomlinson & Dorling, 2016). In the context of decades of uneven development and growing inequality, leading politicians and the right-wing media could pinpoint European integration and the EU as the principal agents responsible for a perceived loss of control focused particularly on immigration and the control of national borders. The combination of forces that came together to support Brexit highlighted the contradictory relationship between neo-liberalism and Euroscepticism. This combined a hyper-liberal globalism, that presented the EU as a regulatory obstacle to the global ambitions of British capitalism, and a popular right-wing nationalism, which demanded state action in response to the transnational forces that were impacting negatively on the material reality of the marginalized and forgotten 'left behind'. The mantra of 'take back control' takes on radically different meanings in these libertarian and conservative contexts and highlights the 'strange bedfellows' within the Leave coalition.

THE STRANGE BEDFELLOWS OF BREXIT:
MARKET FUNDAMENTALISM AND THE RADICAL
RIGHT REACTION

Brexit marks the return of market idealism, but in the context of populist demands for state intervention and protectionism (Worth, 2017). This highlights the Janus-faced nature of the appeal of Brexit, and why a popular Brexit may prove ultimately impossible to deliver. The dominant voices in the Leave campaign were free market idealists, and many were the first-wave intellectual Stormtroopers of Thatcherism from the 1970s and 1980s. Patrick Minford headed *Economists for Brexit*. Nigel Lawson emerged post-Brexit to announce that Brexit would complete the Thatcherite revolution. Founder members of the *Adam Smith Institute* and the *Institute of Economic Affairs* played a prominent role. The post-Brexit cabinet saw the appointment of key libertarian Eurosceptics such as David Davis and Liam Fox. The post-Brexit agenda has been marked by proposals for domestic tax cuts, attracting FDI and the reduction or abolition of corporation tax. The hyper-liberal Euroscepticism includes a commitment to the 'Anglosphere' as an alternative trading bloc to the EU (Wellings & Baxendale, 2105). This sphere includes the United Kingdom, the United States, Australia, Canada and New Zealand and coheres around a common language, history and political culture and a shared set of values (Kenny & Pearce, 2016, p. 304). The notion of the Anglosphere was championed by an influential set of foundations, think-tanks, intellectuals (such as the historian Robert Conquest [see Conquest, 1999]) and media moguls. By the 2010 election, the notion of the Anglosphere had become widely supported in Conservative circles and was cited explicitly in UKIP's 2015 election manifesto. The importance of the Anglosphere is ideological rather than geo-political, as it functions as the imaginary horizon for a Eurosceptic world-view after Brexit that combines a projected global trading future alongside a 'sceptred isle' imagery from Britain's imperial past (Kenny & Pearce, 2016, p. 306).

Brexit also articulated an emergent form of radical right national-populism that appealed to the 'left behind' who supported Brexit because of the socio-economic deprivation and the uncertainties generated by de-industrialization and the 2008 financial crisis. The neo-liberal project of 'market fundamentalism' and the financialization of the global economy resulted in unfettered credit creation, high real rates of interest and the volatility of capital flows across borders. The resulting imbalances were accompanied by policies that encouraged the privatization of state assets, the flexibilization of labour and the suppression of wages (Pettifor, 2017, pp. 127–128). While the development of Euroscepticism amongst elites was ideologically-led, Euroscepticism amongst these groups also had a material basis and was linked to the stagnating incomes and state-induced austerity that followed the 2008 crisis (Lakner & Milanovic, 2013). It was also linked to the perception that high levels of EU immigration had impacted negatively on labour markets and communities. The impact of government-induced austerity, and the further expansion of insecure and degraded employment, combined with the perceived and real impact of immigration on local labour markets to generate a toxic mix that contributed support for Brexit (O'Reilly et al., 2016, pp. 819–820). Employment status was closely correlated to support for Brexit: low-skilled workers with low levels of formal education and training voted 70-30% to leave, while the highest-skilled voted 32-68% to leave (YouGov, 2016). Similarly, the lowest earners voted 66-34% to leave compared to 38-62% amongst the highest earners (Swales, 2016, p. 8). While hyper-liberalism and popular right nationalism appear as strange ideological bedfellows, their joint manifestation following the 2008 crisis highlights the limits and contradictions of market fundamentalism (Soros, 1998).

The 2008 crisis undermined both the ideology of globalization and the economic reality of liberal finance. There is evidence that financial flows have to some extent been domesticated and trade flows have contracted. Indeed, global financial flows collapsed between 2007 and 2009, and remain below pre-crisis levels at around the degree of globalization that existed in 1983 (Pettifor, 2017, p. 128). The crisis resulted in the emergence of oppositional nationalist and protectionist movements demanding that controls be imposed on the global economy. Despite the free market phantasies of neo-liberal globalists, Brexit seems to indicate the beginning of the end for neo-liberalism or perhaps the start of a return to 'organized capitalism' (Nölke, 2017). Brexit articulated a rejection of cosmopolitanism and a demand for a stronger role for the state against the liberalizing forces of globalization. The Brexit vote can be interpreted as part of a broader questioning of the institutional architecture of global neo-liberal capitalism. This is evident from the failed and stalled WTO trade agenda in the Cancun and Doha rounds and the attempt to resuscitate the so-called 'Singapore issues' of competition, investment, procurement and trade facilitation through inter-regional agreements such as the Trans-Atlantic Trade and Investment Partnership (TTIP).

Brexit exposed the fragility and futility of the attempt to build markets beyond the reach of regulatory democracy. The populist reaction to market fundamentalism can be anticipated in the work of Karl Polanyi (2001), who argued that the utopian ideal of a global market, detached from political, social and cultural relations, would mobilize powerful counter-movements from both the right and the left. Brexit represented the collective efforts of the 'left behind' to protect

themselves from the predatory nature of market fundamentalism: a form of self-protection from self-regulating markets in
money, trade and labour (Pettifor, 2017, p. 131). Polanyi
argued that reactionary ideas do not disappear with the
strengthening of the market, but in the 19th century a set of
'double-movements' emerged as state and civil society
attempted to re-regulate in response to the anarchy of the
market. Brexit is part of a 'double movement' against contemporary neo-liberal capitalism. Andreas Nölke (2017) suggests that an emerging model of 'organized capitalism' can be
contrasted with the 'dis-organized capitalism' (Lash & Urry,
1987) of the neo-liberal era, and is defined by a situation in
which companies are part of a quasi-public infrastructure
constrained by institutionally sanctioned collective interests
(Höpner, 2007, pp. 6–7). Organized capitalism can be
either reactionary or progressive. The Brexit vote may lead
to a political economy that is xenophobic, nationalist and
authoritarian or one marked by re-industrialization and
social reform. The resurgence of the Labour Party under
the leadership of Jeremy Corbyn highlights that both radical left and radical right trajectories of 'organized capitalism' remain viable and possible in the post-Brexit context.
It is something of a paradox that, while hyper-globalist
libertarians financed and orchestrated the Leave campaign,
their vision of a post-Brexit economic future is probably
the least viable, because of the forms of popular nationalism that were nurtured, encouraged and exploited by UKIP
and the Leave campaigns.

SUMMARY AND CONCLUSION

In this chapter, I have traced the long pre-history of Brexit in
its broadest structural context. The geo-politics of European

integration were defined by the attempt to maintain the United Kingdom as a 'world power' in the post-war period. This defined the peripheral status of the United Kingdom to European integration, and the crisis of the post-colonial British state generated changing and contentious definitions of 'Britain', 'Britishness' and 'Europe' that framed ambivalent or negative narratives towards European integration. The peripheral status of the United Kingdom to European integration was also determined by the financialization of the British economy and the financial pre-eminence of the City of London. This created a structural mismatch between the trajectories of the British and Continental economies, and the de-industrialization of the British economy leading to the polarization of incomes and wealth and increasing levels of marginalization and insecurity in British society. The state projects of Thatcherism and New Labour were 'passive revolutions' that attempted to encourage the dynamism of the financialized economy, maintain the status of the United Kingdom as a 'world power' and maintain active consent within British society through ideological discourses that continued to highlight British exceptionalism. These state projects both encouraged the intensification of Euroscepticism in British society and shaped the beliefs and identities of the middle-class and working-class support base for Brexit. The 2008 financial crisis resulted in a further intensification of Eurosceptical beliefs and attitudes. In the context of established Eurosceptic discourses, and the impact of the Eurozone crisis and increasing levels of EU immigration, the resulting anxieties and grievances were projected onto the EU as the 'other', responsible for declining opportunities and life chances. This found expression in forms of popular right-wing 'resentful nationalism' orchestrated successfully by UKIP and the Leave campaigns. The Brexit coalition was constituted by an alliance of libertarians and conservatives, and remains contradictory and unstable in the post-Brexit era. In the following chapter, I explore in more detail the socio-cultural dynamics that underpinned the growth and expression of this Euroscepticism, and how this resulted in support for Brexit.

CHAPTER THREE

TWO TRIBES? THE WINNERS AND LOSERS OF EUROPEAN INTEGRATION

In the aftermath of the referendum result many commentators put forward a version of the 'two tribes' interpretation of Brexit. This suggested that the two sides in the referendum campaign represented opposing cultures marked by dominant and subaltern identities. The Remain supporters were the 'winners' in contemporary society, associated with the cultural values of cosmopolitan liberalism and multiculturalism. For this tribe, the EU was vital for expanding educational and career opportunities, EasyJet leisure opportunities and a source of cheap and flexible labour for public and private services. The Leave supporters were the 'losers' in contemporary society, defined by the values of communitarianism, nativism and patriotism. For this tribe, the EU represented a threat, as EU migrants competed for jobs, housing and public services and threatened values and cohesion in already marginalized and declining communities. This story is compelling in its simplicity and tends to confirm the Manichean nature of the

Brexit debate and its representation in the popular media. The notion that Brexit marks the revolt of 'ordinary', 'decent' and 'patriotic' people against a 'privileged' and 'unpatriotic' elite is, of course, a convenient story for the political elites and millionaire hedge-fund managers who orchestrated the Leave campaigns, and this interpretation of Brexit is repeated *ad nauseam* on the pages of the *Daily Express* and the *Daily Mail*. The other problem with this approach is that it tends to present an analysis of Brexit from the perspective of the disappointed and disgruntled 'winners', who ended up on the losing side of the Brexit referendum. This can easily lead to the scapegoating of the 'losers' who supported Brexit.

This process of scapegoating often pinpoints the 'white working class' as the group in society responsible for Brexit. This has resulted in lazy and often vindictive explanations, which present Brexit as being caused by the 'backward' and 'racist' views of the 'white working class', who were either too 'stupid', or too blinded by 'prejudice', to recognize their 'true' economic interests. This type of analysis tends to ignore the real anger and alienation that existed in marginalized communities, and masks the extent to which support for Brexit could be a rational and reasonable decision linked to real inequalities and injustices. The focus on the 'white working class' also downplays the significance of middle-class supporters of Brexit who, in terms of absolute number of votes, were more significant than working-class supporters. In this chapter, I present a critical exploration of the 'two tribes' explanation of Brexit. A significant fragment of the 'white English working class' did indeed vote for Brexit, and this reflected a range of material and cultural issues that went far beyond opposition to the EU. But Brexit was more than a working-class revolt (cf. Harris, 2016) or a working-class revolt manipulated by a cunning and duplicitous segment of the neo-liberal elite (cf. Mason, 2016). How do we explain working-class support for Remain in Scotland and Northern Ireland, where post-industrialization has also bitten hard? Or the significant minority of British Asians that voted in support of Brexit? There were significant sections of the middle class and fragments of the economic and political elites who supported Brexit based on support for either libertarian free market cosmopolitanism, post-imperial jingoism, reactionary nativism or a complex and contradictory combination of all three. The socio-cultural dynamics underpinning Brexit are complex, and cannot be reduced to the simple 'two tribes' argument.

'OTHERING' THE EU: BREXIT AND THE POLITICIZATION OF ENGLISHNESS NATIONALISM

The question of identity was central to determining both support for and opposition to Brexit. The perceived impact of EU membership on British identities was particularly important. This was reflected in the 2015 *British Social Attitudes Survey*, which indicated that 49% of respondents agreed that membership of the EU was undermining Britain's 'distinctive identity' (NatCen Social Research, 2017). The position of respondents on this question of identity proved to be the most important predictor of support for, or opposition to, Brexit: 80% of the respondents who agreed with the proposition signalled their intention to vote Leave, and 89% of those that disagreed signalled their intention to support Remain (Curtice, 2016, p. 6). The relationship between national identity and Euroscepticism has become particularly pronounced in England, and this is significant as the population of England constitutes 85% of the UK population. In contrast, Euroscepticism has declined in Scotland. In the 1975 referendum, support for remaining in the EEC was 68.7% in

England compared to 58.4% in Scotland. In the 2016 referendum, this had been reversed, as strong support for Remain emerged in Scotland (65.6%) compared to 50.4% in England (Henderson et al., 2016, p. 190). These changes in levels of Euroscepticism between the constituent nations of the United Kingdom emerged around the time of the Maastricht Treaty, and have since become more negative in England and less negative in Scotland and Northern Ireland. Since the mid-1990s, Eurosceptic orientations have become the majority position in England. Following the 2008 financial crisis, there was a further increase in Euroscepticism in England; particularly in the Midlands and the South (excluding London) (Henderson et al., 2016, p. 193). These changes were clearly related to the strengthening and politicization of English identity. Survey evidence has indicated that individuals who feel strongly or exclusively English are more likely to have negative attitudes towards the EU compared to individuals who feel strongly or exclusively British. In Scotland, individuals who define themselves as strongly or exclusively British are more likely to have negative views on the EU than individuals who define themselves as Scottish (Henderson et al., 2016, p. 197). The meaning of 'Englishness' and 'Scottishness' and the effects of English and Scottish nationalism lead in opposite directions with regard to orientations towards the EU.

There has never been a strong cultural affinity between the British and the EU that could be expressed in the form of a 'European identity'. In the referendum campaign, Remain campaigners in England found it difficult to articulate a cultural case for EU membership, and this allowed the Leave campaign to dominate the cultural dimension of the debate. In 2012, a Eurobarometer survey highlighted that only 42% of UK citizens considered themselves to be citizens of the EU. This was the lowest across the EU28, and contrasted with an

EU28 average of 61% and significantly higher levels in France (65%), the Netherlands (60%) and Germany (74%) (European Commission, 2012). In the United Kingdom, the dominant orientation towards the EU has, until recently, been ambivalence or indifference, rather than outright Europhobia or Europhilia (Henderson et al., 2016, p. 198). However, individuals with exclusive identities, whether British, English, Welsh or Scottish, tended to be more Eurosceptic than individuals with 'nested identities' – such as a 'nested' English–British–European identity. This is important as there has been a decline in the number of people in the United Kingdom who see themselves as having a 'nested identity' (Bechhofer & McCrone, 2009), and this has coincided with the growth of an exclusive and increasingly politicized English identity that cuts across and undermines established party political alignments and articulates a strong Euroscepticism (Kenny, 2016; Wellings, 2010).

The British state has become increasingly 'de-centred' or 'hollowed out' by European integration, on the one hand, and the devolution of Scotland, Wales and Northern Ireland on the other, and this has generated an English 'resistance identity' (Castells, 1997). The historical development of English nationalism and the category of 'Englishness' involved categories of belonging that were wider than the territorial and cultural boundaries of England, and encompassed the United Kingdom, the Empire and often the global 'Anglosphere' (Dodd, 1986; Wellings & Baxendale, 2015). In the post-war period, the alignment of British and English identity became increasingly problematic, as waves of immigration from former colonies generated hyphenated 'black' British identities such as British-Indian and British-Pakistani (Hall, 1992, p. 310). This resulted in the development of both cosmopolitan multiculturalism and a reactive English nationalism or aggressive 'Little Englandism' (Hall, 1992, p. 308).

The hollowing out of British cultural identity has been intensified by the emergence of Scottish, Welsh and Irish subnationalisms, and the subsequent devolution of Scotland, Wales and Northern Ireland. Simultaneously, the processes of globalization and European integration have generated categories of belonging beyond the nation state. These dynamics generated a form of political Englishness that articulated a defence of British sovereignty and, given the broader contextual factors discussed in chapter two, translated easily into the politics of Euroscepticism (Wellings, 2012).

During the 1970s, the politics of accession to the EU, and the 1975 referendum on membership of the EEC, fused parliamentary and popular sovereignty and heightened the potential threat of European integration to English identity and nationhood. The politics of Thatcherism added an individualistic dimension to the nascent English nationalism and further intensified its Eurosceptical reference points. The resulting anti-European ideology was framed by a popular vision of the past that saw 'Europe' as the ultimate institutional expression of British and English decline. In this context, the category of 'Englishness' became increasingly politicized, as the master frame of 'fairness' was applied to the representation of the English within the United Kingdom, the impact of immigration on English society and the dilution of national sovereignty by European integration (Wyn Jones, Henderson, & Wincott, 2012). A post-imperial sense of loss and disenchantment was intensified by the economic and existential insecurity created by decades of neo-liberal and post-industrial restructuring. The rise of English nationalism, and the marginalization of significant sections of the English working class, generated a potent form of identity politics at a time when established forms of British identity were being challenged by globalization, multiculturalism and devolution. This highlights the importance of post-imperial identity as an important dynamic in the movement towards Brexit and the historical and cultural origins of the 'Anglosphere' as a post-Brexit Eurosceptic fantasy that links Britain's imperial past with its post-Brexit future (Wellings, 2002).

The strengthening of political Englishness is useful in explaining why Euroscepticism is stronger in England than in Scotland or Northern Ireland, and why the possible secession of Scotland, and the nationalist politics of the Scottish National Party (SNP), have become such contentious mobilizing issues in England (Kenny, 2016; Wyn Jones et al., 2013). In Scotland, support for the EU rests upon the vital role of the EU in securing Scottish independence and, in Northern Ireland, the EU mediates the tense relationship with the Irish Republic (Tombs, 2016). The growth of English nationalism is not, however, a direct cause of Euroscepticism. English nationalism articulates a 'resistance identity' to the deep-seated changes in British state and society that are a result of globalization, neo-liberalism and post-industrialization. The legitimation crises of European nation states have generated frustration and fear that has been projected in paranoid ways onto 'others' (Bauman, 2004). Within Continental Europe, migrants and asylum seekers have been 'othered' as 'strangers', as they generate feelings of existential ambivalence within 'Fortress Europe' (Bauman, 1991). In the United Kingdom, the frustrations of post-imperial decline have increasingly been projected onto the 'strangers' that live across the English Channel and populate the headquarters of the EU in Brussels. These feelings of frustration are usually associated with the 'left behind', but who are the 'left behind' and to what extent can this concept contribute to an understanding of the main dynamics and developments leading to Brexit?

NEWS FROM NOWHERE! WHO ARE
THE 'LEFT BEHIND'?

The referendum decision to Brexit was not expected, even by
the Leave campaign, and seemed to emerge from nowhere.
The views and interests of the liberal elites seemed to have
been spurned by a hidden and forgotten segment of the population that have since become known as the 'left behind'. The
'left behind' have become central characters in the Brexit
story, and tend to play a rather teleological role as both the
marginal group responsible for Brexit and an explanation as
to why this group exists and supported Brexit. The category
can throw useful light onto the support base of Brexit, but
only if this type of teleological approach is avoided and the
category is carefully related to the social and cultural dynamics underpinning Brexit. The 'left behind' concept has been
applied in three main ways to the question of how marginalized groups and individuals contributed support for Brexit.
First, the concept has been used in an ideologically loaded
and teleological way, mainly by Remain-supporting cosmopolitan liberals, to scapegoat marginalized individuals and
communities based on their presumed backwardness and
prejudice to blame them for Brexit and explain why the 'left
behind' voted against their own economic interests. Second,
critical commentators have questioned the scapegoating and
stigmatization of the 'left behind' and drawn attention to the
acute levels of material deprivation and hopelessness that are
faced by marginalized groups and hence the anger and frustration, rather than 'stupidity' and 'prejudice' underpinning
support for Brexit amongst marginal groups. Third, there
have been attempts to highlight the narrowness of class-based
definitions of the 'left behind', and to argue that the concept
describes a cultural disposition framed by disappointment of
the way that everyday life is lived and a sense of uneasiness

about the future. In this approach, the 'left behind' is a state of mind rather than a segment of the population in defined locations. This helps to explain the extent of support for Brexit amongst intermediate and middle-class strata of British society, who are subject to feelings of relative deprivation and existential uneasiness, rather than abject material deprivation. I will explore this debate in more detail and argue that a synthesis of the second and third approaches provides a useful framework for understanding the relationship between Brexit, marginalization and identity.

In the first approach, the 'left behind' is shorthand for those Brexit-supporting individuals and groups in British society who perceive themselves to have lost out in the decades of post-industrial and neo-liberal restructuring. The 'left behind' are often equated with the 'white working class'. This is an ideologically loaded term that posits the existence of a static, marginalized and ethnically uniform group upon whom economic decline and multiculturalism have been imposed, and whose values have been shaped by material deprivation and opposition to immigration and multiculturalism. This group is seen to inhabit areas in the vaguely defined 'North' of England, which were formerly dominated by mining, manufacturing and heavy engineering, and now suffer declining life chances and opportunities. The economic and geographical marginalization of the 'left behind' is presumed to be connected to a world outlook that is conservative, communal and patriotic in a world where the dominant values are liberal, cosmopolitan and multicultural. Clearly, the geography of de-industrialization and informationalization highlights how social and economic polarization declining life chances and a sense of marginalization and hopelessness have impacted large swathes of Britain, but is the close and clear correlation between material deprivation and cultural disposition really as neat as this explanation suggests?

Following the referendum, the discourse of the 'left behind' was used to locate the marginalized sections of the working class that had voted for Brexit. The extent to which this can lead to scapegoating and stigmatization is clear, if one considers the venom that was directed against supporters of Brexit by Remain supporters in the wake of the referendum. The sneering condescension tended to imply that Leave supporters had voted against their own economic interests on the basis of 'ignorance', 'stupidity' and 'prejudice'. The referendum did indeed highlight traces of racism and xenophobia amongst many Leave supporters (Khaleeli, 2016), but equally a sense of entitlement, privilege and social hierarchy amongst many Remain supporters (Kibasi, 2016, p. 13). The 'freedoms' to travel, live and work across the Continent, so cherished by many Remain supporters, were empty freedoms for some marginalized Leave supporters and, indeed, experienced by many Leave supporters as a cost to their expected life chances. In this context, the Leave vote of the 'left behind' can perhaps be seen as destructive vote for disruption amongst groups of individuals who really had nothing to lose and were, therefore, immune to dire warnings of economic apocalypse coming from the 'Project Fear' Remain campaign. Or, as Tom Kibasi (2016, pp. 13–14), Director of the *Institute for Public Policy Research* think-tank, has argued, the referendum provided an opportunity for these marginalized groups to impose their reality on the rest of the country, and to reclaim an element of self-respect and dignity in the process. The scapegoating approach underplays the lack of economic opportunities amongst the 'left behind' that may have induced a perfectly 'logical' vote for Brexit amongst marginalized groups, but also displays a form of economic determinism that downplays questions of culture and identity, and the ways in which inequality and marginalization dovetailed with emergent forms of English nationalism (Kibasi, 2016, p. 13).

The second approach has focused on the acute levels of material deprivation experienced within 'left behind' communities and the way in which support for Brexit was a product of intense anger, frustration and demoralization in response to disrupted expectations and declining communities. The racism and xenophobia generated within these communities is itself partially determined by the imposition of a sense of victimhood, when racialized labelling discourses such as the 'white working class' are used to describe these communities and are subsequently internalized and reproduced as a racialized subaltern identity. The anger and frustration of Brexit supporters was captured by London School of Economics (LSE) Sociology Fellow Lisa McKenzie (2016) in an ethnographic study of under-privileged Leave voters in London and a de-industrialized former mining area on the Derbyshire-Nottinghamshire border. The study highlighted how a cycle of anger and apathy underpinned support for Brexit, and articulated a shared class anger and a shared understanding of the unfairness and inequalities that underpinned their social positions. The arguments of the Remain campaign did not resonate with the lived experience of these individuals, on an economic, political or emotional level. McKenzie (2017, pp. 204–205) highlights the apathy and lack of enthusiasm of her respondents to the 2015 general election and contrasts this with the enthusiastic levels of interest and engagement displayed in relation to the EU referendum. These individuals believed that voting for Brexit was a way to kick back at an establishment that had ignored and overlooked them, and appeared genuinely offended by middle-class accusations of bigotry, racism and backwardness. McKenzie (2017, p. 201) argues that the decision of these voters to support Brexit is entirely understandable, and that dismissing their opinions and values as 'irrational' and 'xenophobic' ignores how narratives and markers of class have resulted in the problematization of the 'white working class' (Jones, 2016; Skeggs, 2000, 2004). This has resulted in their representation as 'excess' and 'nothing' (Reay, 2007), or as an embarrassing contradiction marked by being 'abject' and 'white' (Haylett, 2000). The attempts by cosmopolitan liberals to understand these voters through notions of backwardness or labels such as the 'left behind' re-evokes the corrosive narratives of a 'feckless' and undeserving poor that dominated the Victorian era (Savage, Cunningham, & Divine, 2015, p. 352). The 'white working class' formulation ignores the complex, inter-ethnic relations that exist in working-class communities, and the resulting sense of 'victimhood' can be used by the radical right as a basis for mobilization and by the left as a rationale for authoritarian policy interventions that tackle 'class' inequality, but only by problematizing multiculturalism and intensifying racial and ethnic tensions in ways that benefit the far right (Hanley, 2017). These notions downplay or ignore the ethnic diversity of the working class and encourage ethnic division and 'othering'.

The third approach suggests that the 'left behind' is based on cultural rather than material divisions and extends, therefore, beyond the most marginalized sections of the working class. In a comparative study of survey data, political scientists Ronald Inglehart and Pippa Norris (2016) argue that contemporary manifestations of political populism are more associated with a 'cultural backlash' against 'cosmopolitan liberalism' than with the effects of economic inequality on marginalized sectors of society. Brexit highlighted important divisions based on values, culture and identity, such as the desirability and effects of multiculturalism, conflicts and disconnections between different forms of national and transnational identity and divergent assessments of the economic and political value of multiple citizenships (Ashcroft & Bevir, 2016, p. 356). The political consensus around multicultural-ism has been placed under strain by a series of events such as 9/11, 7/7 and the broader effects of the 'war on terror', and this has resulted in significant sections of the population equating multiculturalism with a threat to social cohesion and security (Ashcroft & Bevir, 2016, p. 355). In the United Kingdom, there has been a political backlash against multi-culturalism and, in the process, British Muslims have become an object of government and public suspicion (Fekete, 2016). Multiculturalism has been presented as problematic because it allows minorities to prioritize private commitments over civic loyalty in a way that encourages ghettoization and a breakdown of social cohesion. In public discourse, concerns over multiculturalism, security and immigration are often conflated, as in the UKIP 'Breaking Point' poster issued dur-ing the EU referendum. Multicultural, monocultural and even monoethnic identities are increasingly in competition and combine with divergent definitions of 'Britishness' to create an increasingly complex mosaic of identities that are compli-cated further by differences in identity between England, Wales, Scotland and Northern Ireland.

The notion of the 'left behind' is most useful if it is con-ceived as a cultural disposition marked by varying mixtures of deprivation, frustration and uneasiness, and determined by a lack of control over both the material and symbolic organi-zation of everyday life. This disposition can be found across those groups and individuals who find it increasingly difficult to imagine a viable future for themselves in the de-industrial-ized and informationalized world the digital revolution has opened up: a future where knowledge is the principal cur-rency, connectivity is the primary asset and physical geogra-phy, community and nationality are secondary concerns (Runciman, 2016, p. 6). To focus only on the 'absolute deprivation' of the most marginalized sectors of society downplays the importance of the 'relative deprivation' experienced by a broader demographic as a result of globalization, neo-liberalism and state-induced austerity. Relative deprivation emerges from the perceived gap between what people expect out of life and what they actually experience (Runciman, 1966; Walker & Smith, 2002), and a large gap can lead to frustration, aggression and political action (Walker, Wong, & Kretzschmar, 2002). This formulation allows the definition of the 'left behind' to be widened to include the 'squeezed middle' (Parker, 2013) or those segments of the intermediate and middle-class whose status has declined as a result of globalization and austerity (Antonucci, Horvath, Kutiyski, & Krouwel, 2017). This group was marked by intermediate levels of education and self-identified as middle class, but also had negative psycho-social orientations to the world and contributed to a significant proportion of the Brexit vote. The focus on the working class ignores the importance of the middle class in securing the Brexit vote. The middle class contributed 59% overall to the Leave vote, compared with the working class who contributed 24%, and the majority of the working class who were in employment supported Remain (O'Reilly et al., 2016, p. 811). Brexit occurred because of the real anger and despair of the most marginalized sections of the working class dovetailed with a broader cultural uneasiness generated by financialization, technical change and immigration amongst intermediate, middle-class and older groups in society. These dynamics underpinned an English ethno-nationalism that could be effectively shaped and articulated by the politics of UKIP and the Leave campaign. A common refrain amongst Leave supporters both during and after the referendum was: 'I want my country back'! Was Brexit a proxy war for a more fundamental battle over the meaning of Britishness and the values underpinning British culture? The dynamic tension between class, race and nation and its relationship to Brexit can explored further through an investigation of the 'culture war' that came to a head over the issue of immigration during the referendum campaign.

BREXIT AND THE CULTURE WAR: 'UNPATRIOTIC TRAITORS' VERSUS 'STUPID RACISTS'?

Brexit was the ultimate expression of a culture war that had been developing in the United Kingdom over recent decades. The intensity of this culture war was illustrated by the vitriol released during and after the referendum on both sides of the debate: 'Project Hate' versus 'Project Fear'. During the campaign, it was not unusual to hear Remain supporters branded as unpatriotic 'traitors' by supporters of the Leave campaign, and for Leave supporters to be branded as 'stupid', 'gullible', 'prejudiced' and 'racist' by Remain supporters. Both the Leave and Remain campaigns comprised mainly toxic threats, which tended to further intensify feelings of alienation and anger. The levels of vitriol, hatred and anger were particularly intense in relation to some Leave supporters. This culminated in the murder of Labour MP, and Remain supporter, Jo Cox by a right-wing extremist during the referendum campaign. The murderer, Thomas Mair, shouted 'Britain First' as he shot and stabbed Jo Cox and, when he later appeared in court, gave his name as: 'Death to traitors, freedom for Britain'. Expressions of vitriol continued after the referendum, encouraged by the right-wing tabloid media. 'Damn the unpatriotic "bemoaners" and their plot to subvert the will of the British people', screamed the *Daily Mail* on October 12, 2016. The 'Guyana-born' businesswomen Gina Miller, who initiated a Supreme Court review of the Government's decision to trigger Article 50 without a parliamentary review, was subjected to online racial abuse and threats of rape and death. Following the referendum, there was a spike in hate crimes against migrants and ethnic minorities. The *Institute of Race Relations* catalogued over 80 incidents between 24 June and 5 July 2016, including the firebombing of a halal butcher in Walsall, graffiti on a Polish community centre in London and laminated cards reading 'No more Polish vermin' posted through letterboxes in Huntingdon (IRR, 2016).

The racist incidents that occurred following the referendum have been described by sociologist Paul Bagguley as 'celebratory racism'. This involved some Leave supporters 'expressing a sense of power and success that they have won' (Bagguley quoted in Khaleeli, 2016). This highlighted the enduring existence of the one-third of the British population that hold intolerant views, and whose opinions appeared vindicated by the Brexit vote. This emboldened individuals to openly expound views that they would previously have kept to themselves: 'the unspeakable, became not only speakable, but commonplace' (Keith quoted in Chakrabortty, 2016). This was encouraged by the Leave campaign slogans of 'controlling our borders' and 'we want our country back', which served to demonized immigrants and define them as an alien presence that needed to be expelled. The 'keyboard race warriors' shifted the battleground from Facebook, online blogs and media comment boards, to real-life verbal and physical confrontation and abuse. Examples of this included a Muslim schoolgirl cornered by a group of people who told her: 'Get out, we voted Leave!'. Or the case of Eastern Europeans stopped from using the London Underground with shouts of: 'Go back to your own country!' (Versi, 2016). Many attacks were inspired by a false belief that EU citizens would be forced to immediately leave the United Kingdom following the Brexit vote. Examples include a Polish woman told to get off a bus in Manchester and to: 'Get packing!' (Lyons, 2016). Support for the British National Party (BNP) has declined since 2010, and these developments highlight how UKIP was able to capture and mobilize the 'respectable racist' vote, and how the Leave campaign legitimized expressions of racism by aligning the politics of the EU with the politics of immigration.

The decision to Brexit was intimately related to the 'rise of the right' in British politics (Winlow, Hall, & Treadwell, 2017). Over the past two decades, a range of right-wing parties have developed in the United Kingdom: including the BNP, English Defence League (EDL), Britain First, the English Democrats and UKIP. In the early 2000s, the BNP made significant electoral advances in local authority and European elections, but the rise of UKIP tended to marginalized the BNP and other parties of the far-right. The replacement of the abrasive and boorish Nick Griffin, with the blazer-clad, affable and 'bloke-down-the-pub'-like Nigel Farage as principal mouthpiece of the radical right, furnished UKIP with a veneer of political respectability that the BNP, with its associations with street-fighting skinheads, tattooed football hooligans and *Combat 18*, was never able to achieve. UKIP narrowed the agenda of the far right onto Europe, and in doing so widened its electoral appeal. The rise of the right has been linked to the toxic combination of material deprivation, political alienation from metropolitan liberal elites and a melancholic sense of hopelessness at the loss of 'imagined' working-class communities in the post-industrial heartlands. This has resulted in a growth of Islamophobia and the scapegoating of Muslims and other immigrants who are seen as responsible for this sense of loss and decline (Winlow et al., 2017). The resulting increase in racism has been compounded by the way mainstream political parties have approached the issues of race and immigration. The state-sponsored Islamophobia associated with the prevention of Islamic extremism has fused neo-liberalism and authoritarian nationalism (Fekete, 2016). The Conservative Party has used Islamophobia for electoral advantage; as highlighted in the 2016 mayoral election in London when there was an attempt to link the Labour Party candidate, Sadiq Khan, to a radical imam with supposed links to Islamic State of Iraq and the Levant (ISIL). The defensiveness of the Labour Party on the issue has led to occasional pandering to racist sentiment or the avoidance of debate and discussion on the topic. These developments provided legitimation for the expression of racist views and opinions. In the May 2014 European elections, UKIP finished in first place with 26.6% of the vote and, by 2014, the Party become the most popular choice amongst its core constituency of older, white, working-class men. This was to translate into a significant constituency of support for Brexit.

Clearly, not all Leave supporters were racist, and intolerant views and opinions were present amongst a significant segment of the British population. But the referendum provided both a context in which latent forms of racism could surface, and highlighted how these latent forms had been intensified by the impact of austerity, a rapid increase in immigration and a wide-scale perception that mainstream politicians had been misleading and incompetent in the management of immigration and the 2008 financial crisis. The start of this process can be traced to the policies of New Labour between 1997 and 2010. New Labour pursued finance-led neo-liberal economic policies, which included support for the eastward expansion of the EU and a liberal approach to immigration from the new East European accession states. At the same time, New Labour suppressed debate and discussion on the level and impact of immigration (Woolas, 2010), and this generated an increasing disconnect between New Labour and its core supporters. An illustration of this was the encounter between Prime Minister Gordon Brown and Gillian Duffy, a Labour supporter from Rochdale, during the 2010 general election campaign, who Brown described as a 'bigot' after she questioned him on the economic effects of immigration (Curtis, 2010). The demographic consequences of New Labour policies were particularly important (Coleman, 2016). New Labour lacked a coherent or explicit 'immigration policy', which reflected a concern that the issue could cause electoral damage to the Party and a tendency within the Party to conflate the issues of 'immigration' and 'race'. The latter reflected the long-term commitment of the Party to promoting racial equality, and an assumption that discussing immigration would stir up racist sentiments. Consequently, New Labour's approach to immigration tended to be 'reactive, defensive and weak', and this tended to fuel public mistrust (Owen, 2010, pp. 15–16). There was, however, an underlying New Labour assumption that immigration would be made fairer and that increasing immigration would be good for economic competitiveness and growth in the context of an aging population (Spencer, 2010).

New Labour started to challenge the uneasy political consensus that had developed around immigration, which had accepted the need to limit inflows of migrants and which had kept net annual migration to around 40,000. In 1997, New Labour removed the 'primary purpose rule', designed to filter out fake marriage applications. The new policy provoked a rapid surge in migration, and immigration had already reached record levels when New Labour decided to allow free entry to migrants from the eight new Eastern European accession countries (the A8). In all other EU nations, except Ireland and Sweden, transitional controls were established. The A8 had markedly different levels of income and wealth to the existing EU15, and these proved to be important 'push' factors for immigration into the United Kingdom. The number of A8 migrants living in the United Kingdom increased from 167,000 in 2004 to 998,000 in 2011. By 2013, 1.24 million people born in Central and Eastern Europe were living in the United Kingdom. There was no forward planning for this influx, as the Government had predicted that only 13,000 Eastern European migrants would enter each year, and this started to impact negatively on housing, schools and the National Health Service (NHS). There was also a significant increase in migration from other EU nations, such as Portugal, and migration from outside the EU. Between 2001 and 2014, 3.3 million immigrants entered the United Kingdom. The 2011 census showed that 2.7 million EU citizens were resident in the United Kingdom, with 1.1 million of these being from the post-2004 member states. Migration accounted for 85% of population growth between 2001 and 2012 (see Coleman, 2016, for detailed breakdown of demographic statistics).

The defeat of New Labour in 2010 reflected the Party's poor handling of the economy following the 2008 financial crisis and the mismanagement of immigration (Ford & Somerville, 2010, pp. 10–11). The incoming Coalition was led by the Conservative Party, which had pledged, in its 2010 manifesto, to cut immigration to 'tens of thousands per year' through an annual limit on immigration, new curbs on unskilled workers, and 'transitional controls' on new European Union member states (Conservative Party, 2010, p. 21). In the context of EU rules on the free movement of labour, this proved impossible and immigration continued to increase. Between 2013 and 2014, the population of the United Kingdom increased by 491,000 or 0.77% (Coleman, 2016). The Coalition abandoned the 'one nation' legitimation strategy of New Labour for a 'two nations' legitimation strategy, which continued the finance-led neo-liberal accumulation strategy alongside, austerity, welfare cuts and a squeeze on wage levels. This legitimation strategy was underpinned by a discourse that distinguished between the deserving and undeserving poor in terms of 'strivers' and 'skivers', and this encouraged a 'moralized' antagonism between different groups in society (Lavery, 2017, pp. 8–10). The result of these developments was an increasingly toxic political culture that disconnected and alienated large parts of the United Kingdom from political elites who were increasingly represented as dishonest, sleazy and corrupt. This was reflected in declining voter turnout and declining levels of support for mainstream political parties, alongside increasing levels of anger, resentment and frustration and the growing support for the radical right project articulated by UKIP. The disconnected masses were ultimately to find their voice in the decision to Brexit, but much of the energy of this movement derived from the effects of austerity and the perceived mishandling of immigration policy by successive governments.

THE END OF THE PHONEY WAR: 'RESENTFUL NATIONALISM' AND THE POLITICS OF 'POST-LIBERALISM'

The combination of post-crisis austerity and a rapid increase in immigration created a situation in which large swathes of the British population experienced varying combinations of economic and cultural insecurity. This provided an opportunity for UKIP to enter on the popular right of British politics and articulate a form of 'resentful nationalism' (Condor & Fenton, 2012; Fenton, 2012; Mann & Fenton, 2009; Seymour, 2015, p. 35). This is a form of nationalism that is common when personal decline has a 'class trajectory', often in a context in which 'lived decline' is marked on the lived environment – for example areas blighted by the collapse of mining, docking, steel, fishing and textiles. When class is used primarily as a moralizing or stigmatizing discourse, in forms such as the 'white working class' or the 'underclass', this can reinforce a sense of victimhood and claims for national entitlement and priority. These dynamics clearly underpinned the growing popularity of UKIP following the 2008 crisis. The long-term dynamics of deindustrialization and financialization were reinforced by the impact of the 2008 crisis to produce increasing levels of inequality, insecurity and anxiety. This occurred alongside a significant increase in immigration, and in a political environment in which debate on immigration was stifled. The language of class had been removed from the political lexicon, except as a moralizing and demonizing label applied to the dissolute 'chavs' and 'skivers' who were seen to inhabit the post-industrial wastelands, decaying council estates and the stage of the TV talk show, *The Jeremy Kyle Show*. This provided a perfect breeding ground for forms of 'resentful nationalism', which could be captured and articulated by the radical right politics of UKIP.

Case studies have demonstrated how deindustrialization fused with the crisis of social democracy in the post-industrial heartlands to generate populist support for UKIP and ultimately for Brexit. An interesting attempt to explore these dynamics can be found in an anthropological study of post-industrial decline and support for UKIP in Doncaster, carried out by Norwegian anthropologist Cathrine Moe Thorleifsson in 2016. Doncaster is a town in South Yorkshire that has been negatively impacted by neo-liberal restructuring and post-industrial decline following the decline of the coal industry in the 1980s and 1990s. This resulted in high levels of unemployment and economic insecurity, and economic diversification resulted in the inward migration of workers from Central and Eastern Europe. While the town retains two

Labour MPs, support for UKIP increased over the past decade and in the referendum 69% voted for Brexit. In times of existential insecurity, nostalgia can function as a potent source of social reconnection and identity (Strathern, 1995, p. 111), and in Doncaster, Thorleifsson encountered a nostalgia for the lost feelings of community once associated with the 'affect factory' of the coalmines and the tight-knit and homogenous residential areas that radiated from these 'Fordist' workplaces (Muehlebach & Shoshan, 2012, p. 318). The decline of coal mining not only resulted in a loss of employment, but undermined the activities that gave people a sense of community, identity, certainty, friendship and dignity (Thorleifsson, 2016, p. 557). Deindustrialization generated forms of existential insecurity that proliferated melancholic narratives about the past, enforced cultural stereotypes and strengthened ethnic nationalism. This English nationalism articulated the threat of an invading 'other', which threatened established notions of national culture through a discourse of bio-social purity, culture and 'roots' (Gullestad, 2006), and resulted in a re-imagined sense of Englishness (Anderson, 2006). This took the specific form of an exclusionary and resentful 'coal nationalism', which articulated demands for the strengthening of symbolic and geographical borders, and dovetailed effectively with the anti-migration and anti-EU politics of UKIP and support for Brexit.

The grievances and resentments generated by financialization and the 2008 crisis, however, extended far beyond post-industrial areas such as Doncaster and, in a political culture conducive to radical right populism, UKIP could mobilize a significant cross-class alliance of 'resentful nationalists'. These developments in the United Kingdom are part of a broader phenomenon of political realignment, and throughout Europe right-wing populist parties and movements have developed

(Greven, 2016; Mudde, 2009), alongside a protracted crisis of social democracy and declining support for centre right Christian democratic and conservative parties. The new populist parties combine 'right-wing' positions on questions of identity and social cohesion and 'left-wing' positions on welfare and the economy (Pabst, 2016, p. 189). Following the 2008 economic crisis, questions of substantive justice reemerged and were articulated by sections of society that were marginalized by the social liberal consensus. The new politics was defined by greater focus on economic egalitarianism and a renewed (small c) conservatism (Pabst, 2016, p. 190). These developments highlight how 'post-liberalism' has become the new centre ground of British politics, and the ways in which the culture war is defined by a struggle between post-liberal and libertarian forms of identity (Pabst, 2016). This encouraged the 'two tribes' thesis of Brexit, which posits that the EU referendum campaign was a battle fought between nativist post-liberal supporters of Leave and cosmopolitan liberal or libertarian supporters of Remain. The socio-cultural dynamics underpinning Brexit were, however, more complex and the divide between liberals and post-liberals cut across the opposition between Leavers and Remainers. This reflected an emerging 'culture war' between an amoral libertarian liberalism and a small-c conservatism based on the values of tradition, rootedness, community and patriotism (Pabst, 2016, pp. 191–192).

This culture war does not map neatly onto the two sides of the EU referendum debate. In the Tory shires (including small towns) and across suburbia, many fractions of both the middle class and working class supported a 'national liberation' Brexit with strong Thatcherite overtones; particularly the baby-boomer generation whose anti-establishment radicalism in the 1960s has since morphed into support for hyper-global free trade and financialization unfettered by EU regulation. This support for Brexit on the Conservative libertarian right was mirrored by some Labour (and former Labour) supporters who supported Brexit from a libertarian left position, which focused on the undemocratic and neoliberal characteristics of the EU (See Tuck, 2016). Support for Brexit was also found amongst those marginalized members of the working class that suffered abject poverty and welfare dependence and a sense of social and cultural alienation from metropolitan liberalism. Similarly, the Remain vote cannot be reduced to the Establishment or cosmopolitan liberal elites, as demonstrated by strong support in London, which is marked by high levels of social capital and extensive religious practice. For example, the majority of British Asians voted to remain in the EU (68−32%), and amongst the minority supporting Brexit, this was often based on cosmopolitan and internationalist concerns regarding the disparity between the position of EU-migrants and migrants from the Indian subcontinent. The Brexit vote does not, therefore, neatly reflect the binary oppositions of metropolitan versus provincial, urban versus rural, rich versus poor, young versus old, business versus workers and north versus south. Political scientist Adrian Pabst (2016, p. 192) argues that post-liberalism is the new centre ground of British politics because libertarians oscillate between abstract cosmopolitanism, economic globalism and ethnic nativism, while post-liberals attempt to fuse patriotism with an internationalist outlook. This oscillation highlights the cultural turbulence that has developed as established identities based on class, ideology, region and religion have weakened and established political alignments have become unstable or collapsed. Political parties have become increasingly 'hollowed out', and disoriented and angry voters have turned to single-issue campaigns or insurgent populism (Tombs, 2017). These factors combined to generate the populist forces that underpinned the growing support for UKIP between 2010 and 2015 and which were manipulated and harnessed by the Leave campaign in the EU referendum.

It is tempting to view the EU referendum campaign as a localized dispute amongst the economic and political elites: a debating society spat between the 'ex-Bullingdon Boys' of the 'Notting Hill Set' who were always going to win whichever side of the argument prevailed. It is, indeed, a paradox that a bunch of over-privileged, middle-aged white men in suits could articulate a form of nationalistic populism that spoke so eloquently to the oppression and victimhood of the marginalized, demoralized and 'left behind'. While the vote for Brexit can perhaps be interpreted as an expression of ambivalence to both sides of the debate (Younge, 2016), the above analysis suggests that this ambivalence goes far deeper than a shared disdain for David Cameron, Boris Johnson and Michael Gove. The Leave campaign prevailed precisely because the populist discourse articulated by the campaign combined a libertarian critique of the EU with a bricolage of cultural reference points that could be combined with cosmopolitanism, economic globalism and ethnic nativism. The fact that Boris Johnson and Michael Gove and other leaders of the Leave campaigns probably did not believe, and certainly did not understand, the populist narratives they tapped into and fuelled, misses the point (cf. Kibasi, 2016, pp. 14–15). The Leave campaign mantras of 'take back control' and 'we want our country back' addressed simultaneously the material and cultural insecurities of the marginalized 'have nots' and declining 'haves' around threats to the welfare state, immigration and the cultural cohesion of local communities and the post-imperial ambitions and phantasies of a significant fragment of the 'have lots'. This was achieved through the skilful interweaving of a narrative that focused on how the EU was undermining the freedom and prosperity of the British people with a narrative focused on how EU migrants were undermining British culture and British identity. This was combined with a 'post-truth' discourse of lies, distortions and misrepresentations and a populist assault on the privileged economic, political and cultural elites leading the Remain campaign. While it is ironic that this populist challenge was led by a section of the elite, it worked because the Remain campaign failed to articulate a viable socio-cultural case for remaining in the EU, but focused narrowly on the dire economic consequences that would follow Brexit. The Leave campaign could skilfully focus the referendum campaign on the question of immigration, rather than the EU, and the economic consequences of Brexit. This worked so effectively because the left had attempted to close down conversations about immigration, identity and integration. The right opened up these conversations and mixed them with a narrative of economic decline and generated a formidable populist force. This force was, however, highly volatile and unstable and continues to disrupt and disturb British state and society in the post-Brexit era.

SUMMARY AND CONCLUSION

The 'two tribes' explanation of Brexit fails to grasp the socio-cultural complexity underpinning Brexit. It tends to encourage lazy and often vindictive forms of analysis in which the blame for Brexit is pinned on the 'left behind', who are often defined in narrow socio-economic terms as the 'white working class', and who are presumed to have supported Brexit because of backward, racist and xenophobic attitudes that were contrary to their own economic interests. This type of analysis tends to downplay the real material deprivation experienced by marginal groups and relies on a form of economic determinism that ignores or downplays the importance of identity and culture in defining orientations towards Brexit. In this chapter I have demonstrated how the emergence of an increasingly politicized form of English national identity informed, and was shaped by, perceptions of marginalization, frustration and loss, as the integrity and meaning of the British state and the cultural cohesion of Britishness as an identity was squeezed between the centripetal forces of devolution within the United Kingdom and the transnational forces of globalization and European integration. The negative effects of the post-2008 austerity programmes and the real and perceived effects of high levels of EU-immigration fused the dynamics of class, race and nation into forms of 'resentful nationalism' that found expression in support for UKIP and Brexit. The 'white working class' in the de-industrialized rustbelts were the most visible manifestation of this process, but the phenomenon extended into the intermediate and middle classes. This suggests that the 'left behind' support for Brexit is most usefully understood as a cultural disposition evoked by relative deprivation and a declining class trajectory than a narrow socio-economic segment of the working class. I concluded by highlighting that, while post-liberalism is the new centre ground of British politics, the post-liberal and libertarian divide does not map neatly onto the two sides of the Brexit debate. Brexit demonstrated the socio-cultural turbulence of post-crisis Britain and the way in which this defines the increasingly populist nature of British politics. The next chapter explores the electoral politics of Brexit in more depth and detail.

CHAPTER FOUR

NEW POLITICAL ALIGNMENTS? THE MAKING OF A PRO-BREXIT ELECTORAL COALITION

Brexit is connected to the wave of populism that is sweeping the contemporary world, and populist movements have emerged on both the left and right of the political spectrum in the period following the 2008 financial crisis (Müller, 2016, pp. 1−4). The populist nature of the Brexit campaign was highlighted in the pronouncements of leading members of the Leave campaign. When the result of the referendum became clear, Nigel Farage, leader of UKIP and prominent member of the Leave campaign, proclaimed, in full populist pomp, the significance of Brexit. Brexit was a victory for 'real people', a victory for 'ordinary people' and a victory for 'decent people' and, above the cheers of his ecstatic supporters, he declared: 'Let June 23rd go down in our history as our Independence Day'. This proclamation reflected the mantras at the heart of the Leave campaigns: 'take back control' and 'we want our country back'. Despite his own privileged background and Establishment credentials, Farage presented himself as an insurgent 'man of the people', stating: 'We have fought against the multinationals, we have fought against the big merchant banks, we fought against big politics, we fought against lies, corruption and deceit' (Walker, 2016). What defines populism is an appeal to a mythologized past and a mythologized people (Marquand, 2017). The 'people', in this formulation, is the undifferentiated and homogenous body of people whose interests are contrasted with and antithetical to the interests of a treacherous, corrupt and subversive elite. The mythologized past is also clear: the age of *Pax Britannica*, when an imperial Britain stood in 'splendid isolation' as a global and European hegemon, or the age of *Dunkirk*, when a plucky 'Little England' stood alone and isolated against the combined might of European tyranny (Hutton, 2017). In this chapter, I present a detailed analysis of why a dynamic form of Eurosceptic populism emerged as such a potent political force following the 2008 financial crisis and became a trailblazer for Brexit.

THE 'EUROPE QUESTION' IN BRITISH POLITICS

The 'Europe question' is related to fundamental questions of national identity and national interpretations of history (Oliver, 2015, p. 413). The United Kingdom was a late-comer to the EEC, and joined following episodes of national humiliation when the UK's application to join was vetoed by France. The negative connotations between the EEC and national pride were compounded by a popular conception that, by joining the EEC, the United Kingdom was abdicating its role as a global power, and abandoning former imperial alliances and markets. The British Empire and the process of post-imperial decline have framed the relationship between the United Kingdom and Europe, and this has resulted in a discourse of British exceptionalism that highlights the distinctiveness of British economic, political and cultural development. On both the political left and the political right, the approach to Europe and membership of European institutions has been either hostile or framed by a sense of instrumental and pragmatic inevitability. The British have been 'reluctant Europeans', rather than keen and committed adherents of the European project of European integration and the goal of 'ever-closer union'. The dominant orientation towards Europe in the United Kingdom has been transactional and instrumental: a means to an end; and the end has always been defined in terms of the 'national interest' and how European integration could benefit the British economy and Britain's political and diplomatic status in the world (Oliver, 2015, p. 413). This has been reflected in public attitudes towards Europe, which have tended to exhibit ambivalence and indifference towards European institutions. In a context of indifference and growing hostility, 'Europe' became increasingly externalized as the 'other' against which British and English identity and history was cast (Oliver, 2015, p. 413). The framing of the 'Europe question' has shifted in response to the shifting ideological terrain of British politics. This has been defined by a shift from One Nation Conservativism to Thatcherism on the right and a shift from revolutionary and reformist labourism to New Labour on the left.

During the post-war period, debates on Europe within the Conservative Party stressed the exceptionalism of UK institutions and development through the ideological lens of One Nation Conservativism. The 'outsider' status of the United Kingdom was highlighted, along with the privileging of Empire, Commonwealth and the 'special relationship' with the United States. This was framed within the tradition of conservative statecraft, which privileged pragmatism and incrementalism over dogma and ideology and, therefore, the decision on whether to support European integration was ultimately based on a pragmatic assessment of how involvement would impact the economic interests of the United Kingdom (Fontana & Parsons, 2015, pp. 90–91). This assessment started to shift from a negative to a more positive orientation as the British economy performed poorly compared to Continental rivals in the 1950s (Fontana & Parsons, 2015; Ludlow, 1997, p. 92). The British Conservative Party and business interests provided the greatest impetus towards UK membership of the EEC; although there were persistent Eurosceptic critics such as Enoch Powell, who opposed the EEC because it would erode British sovereignty, parliamentary democracy and British values, and whose ideas were to be consistently revived in the Thatcher and UKIP eras (Forster, 2002, pp. 38–39; Macshane, 2015, pp. 57–62; Seymour, 2015, p. 36).

During the same period, the Labour Party policy on Europe ranged from indifference to hostility (Macshane, 2015, pp. 35–36). The balance between positive and negative orientations within the Party reflected the changing balance of power between a broadly pro-European right-wing leadership and a broadly anti-European left-wing membership (Callaghan, 2007; Featherstone, 1988; Newman, 1983). In the immediate post-war period, Labour Party leaders were opposed to membership of the ECSC. Hugh Gaitskell, who led the Labour Party during the 1950s, opposed UK entry to the EEC, because it would undermine parliamentary sovereignty and the viability of Keynesian planning. The poor economic performance of the UK economy and the commitment of the Labour Party, under the leadership of Harold Wilson, to modernize the British economy in the 'white heat of the scientific revolution', led to a begrudging support for EEC membership amongst the party leadership (Geddes, 2013, p.55). This resulted in a tension within the party between 'revisionists' and 'statists': the former accepted European integration as an inevitable response to international economic integration and vital to economic modernization, while the latter viewed joining the EEC as a surrender to supranational capitalism (Macshane, 2015, p. 53). Harold Wilson was a 'revisionist', but he was also critical of the EEC terms of entry negotiated by the Conservatives in 1973 and initiated the 1975 referendum. The referendum exposed the fault lines of the Labour Party on Europe: a pro-European right-wing 'revisionism' led by Harold Wilson, Roy Jenkins and Shirley Williams and a left-wing anti-European 'statism' led by Tony Benn, Michael Foot and Barbara Castle.

The events surrounding the Maastricht Treaty and the UK's ejection from the ERM highlighted a critical shift towards Euroscepticism in the Conservative Party. In her Bruges speech in 1988, Margaret Thatcher highlighted a belief in the incompatibility of supranational authority and national democracy, and this discourse started to resonate with a growing segment of the Conservative Party. These developments coincided with an ideological shift from One Nation Conservatism to Thatcherism. The 'One Nation' model of conservatism based on traditionalism, class-based paternalism and a post-war embrace of the social democratic consensus was challenged by a 'free economy — strong state' strategy based on a conviction-led assault on those elements in society that opposed free market liberalism (Gamble, 1994). The shift to conviction politics in the domestic sphere dovetailed with the nascent Euroscepticism in the Conservative Party (Vail, 2014). An aggressive nationalism focused on British independence could be counterpoised against the EU as an embodiment of social solidarity, social cohesion and 'ever-closer union'. This created an increasing tension in the Conservative Party between 'soft' and 'hard'

Euroscepticism and deep divisions within Conservative elites, which resulted in the political downfall of Margaret Thatcher, reverberated through the unstable and fractious Major administration and re-emerged in an even more virulent form when the Conservatives returned to power in 2010.

Meanwhile, following the 1979 election defeat, and under the leadership of Michael Foot, the Labour Party adopted a position of outright opposition to the EEC as a key component of its protectionist 'Alternative Economic Strategy' (AES) (see Aaronovitch, 1981). This reflected a deep Euroscepticism throughout the parliamentary Party, grassroots membership and the trade unions (Forster, 2002, p. 68). In 1981, this led to a split in the Labour Party, as leading pro-Europeans, including Roy Jenkins, Shirley Williams and David Owen, formed the pro-European Social Democratic Party (SDP), and nearly two dozen Labour MPs left to join the breakaway party (Crewe & King, 1995). In the 1983 general election, the Labour Party manifesto called for an immediate withdrawal of the United Kingdom from the EEC. The Labour Party suffered a catastrophic defeat in 1983, and this provided the catalyst for the development of a more pro-European orientation under the leadership of Neil Kinnock, John Smith and Tony Blair. The Europhilic shift was opportunistic, and driven partly by an opportunity to exploit Conservative divisions on Europe, but mainly to marginalize the left within the labour movement. The 'modernization' of the Party was an attempt to create a 'modern' *European* social democratic party that accepted the increasing interdependence of the international economy and embraced international cooperation and solidarity. Under New Labour, there was a 'Europeanization' of party policy and strategy, including an embrace of European institutions and initiatives, such as the single market, the Social Chapter and ERM (Holden, 1999; Ladrech, 1994). Following the

1997 election victory, New Labour granted independence to the Bank of England in preparation for EMU and reversed the opt-out of the Social Chapter.

The 'Europe question' was probably the most contentious issue in post-war British politics. It inflicted a near-fatal split in the Labour Party, and defined decades of internecine struggle within the Conservative Party. The election of New Labour was an important moment as it marked an attempt to de-politicize the 'Europe question'. The 'Europeanization' of the Labour party involved an increasing alignment between the New Labour approach to government and the technocratic and undemocratic institutions of the EU. The EU is a form of de-politicized expert governance constructed to avoid parties, popular democracy and redistributive politics (Mair, 2013). The EU is constitutionally and culturally hostile to democracy, and decades of European integration have institutionalized free market neo-liberalism and insulated the 'four freedoms' from democratic challenge or scrutiny (Carchedi, 2001; Milward, 2000; Streeck, 2014, 2015). The attempt to de-politicize European integration is consistent with the understanding of New Labour as a 'passive revolution': a term developed by Antonio Gramsci to describe a major transformation of the capitalist mode of production to overcome obstacles to accumulation. This type of revolution takes place in a conservative-adaptive way that requires both ideological coercion and active consent (Johnson & Steinberg, 2004, p. 12; Seymour, 2015, p. 37). New Labour achieved this 'passive revolution' by capturing the political centre ground. This involved a rhetorical commitment to progressive liberalism, cosmopolitan inclusivity and 'Europe', while imposing strict discipline through managerial neo-liberalism, the restructuring and intensification of middle-class and public sector employment, public–private partnerships and the restructuring of welfare around employability and individual responsibility (Steinberg & Johnson, 2004). In this context, New Labour became increasingly disconnected from its traditional working-class support base and highlighted the shift towards a new form of party-less, de-politicized democracy (Mair, 2000).

The technocratic approach of New Labour was evident in the 'utilitarian supranationalism' that informed its approach to relations with the EU. This approach involved constructive cooperation in the European integration process, while downplaying the significance of this in the public arena. (Menon & Salter, 2016, p. 1302). New Labour became principally concerned with the need to reform Europe through the 'Third Way' agenda that had been developed in the domestic sphere. This was combined with keen support for Eastward expansion of the EU and led to the technocratic decision not to restrict the entry of A8 migrants from Central and Eastern Europe into the United Kingdom (Watt & Wintour, 2015). The elite-level management of relations with the EU by New Labour intensified media criticisms of the remote, unresponsive and undemocratic nature of the EU, and the 'destructive dissent' and scaremongering that had first developed in the 1980s, became more intense (Daddow, 2012). This resulted in a vicious circle linking technocratic, but politically cautious, parties, a scathing Eurosceptic right-wing press and an ambivalent public. An environment was created where critical Eurosceptical movements and parties could develop and grow. The 1990s saw the emergence of new radical groupings outside the main parties including the Anti-Federalist League, the Referendum Party and UKIP. The New Labour project was to ultimately implode following the 2008 financial crisis and increasing public concerns over the party's management of EU immigration.

Following the defeat of New Labour in 2010, the Conservative-Liberal Democrat Coalition government continued the technocratic orientation towards European integration, but increasingly framed this within a critical Eurosceptical discourse that stressed the dysfunctionality of the EU. The election of David Cameron as leader of the Conservative Party marked a defeat for the Eurosceptic right and middle-class support base within the Party by a pro-business technocrat from the political centre (Seymour, 2015, p. 27). The right did not concede defeat, and Cameron was faced with a party that had become increasingly right-wing and Eurosceptic, and faced an increasingly potent external threat from UKIP (Fontana & Parsons, 2015; Lynch, 2012, p. 100). Cameron attempted to combine a technocratic engagement with the EU with an increasingly hostile and belligerent Euroscepticism designed to ameliorate internal criticism and external threats from UKIP. Cameron withdrew the Conservatives from the *European People's Party* bloc in the European Parliament and aligned with a new right-wing bloc of Eurosceptic parties. This was followed by a pledge that there would be no more transfer of sovereignty to the EU before the following election, and this was protected by the so-called 'referendum lock' enshrined within the 2011 *European Union Act*. Cameron also pledged to reduce levels of EU migration; a pledge that he was not able to fulfil owing to EU rules on the free movement of labour. In 2013, Cameron promised that, if re-elected in 2015, he would establish a 'new settlement' for the United Kingdom in Europe, followed by an in/out referendum. This failed to appease Eurosceptics in the Conservative Party and support for UKIP continued to increase; culminating in UKIP achieving 27.5% of the vote in the 2015 European elections and the defection of Douglas Carswell and Mark Reckless from the Conservatives to UKIP. Cameron articulated a populist anti-EU rhetoric using the vocabulary of the One-Nation nationalist discourse, but did so alongside a stringent neo-liberal economic strategy of austerity that accentuated class divisions and undermined the One-Nation tradition. Cameron demonized the EU rhetorically, while mirroring the German-led economic orthodoxy in practice. The soothing rhetoric of the 'Big Society' paternalism and anti-EU nationalism attempted to mask the validation and imitation of the regressive and divisive neo-liberalism of the EU (Vail, 2014, p. 118). This attempt to balance the tensions between 'hard' and 'soft' Euroscepticism and the One-Nation and Thatcherite traditions within the Conservative Party could not withstand its own internal contradictions. The tensions and contradictions of the main political parties on the EU had opened space for an explicitly anti-EU party and, from 2010 until the Brexit referendum, this space became occupied by UKIP. The attempt to de-politicize and suppress public debate and criticism on the EU had seriously rebounded and it was re-politicized by an insurgent radical right populism following the 2008 financial crisis that would lead ultimately to Brexit.

A MESSAGE FROM THE 'HEARTLAND': BREXIT, POPULISM AND THE RISE OF UKIP

In the aftermath of the 2008 financial crisis, and with growing public discontent over the level and impact of immigration, it became easier to locate the problems facing British society at the door of a corrupt, incompetent and out-of-touch elite that had lied and misled the public over issues such as the Iraq War and immigration, and seemed to have put their own interests before the interests of 'ordinary' people. The declining legitimacy of the mainstream political parties left space for an insurgent right-wing populist party, such as UKIP, to harness these concerns and articulate them as part of a populist assault on elites and, given the quotidian

reality of the EU as a remote, undemocratic, elite-led organization, present the EU and 'Brussels bureaucrats' as an
über-elite with overall responsibility for popular concerns
and grievances. UKIP is a textbook example of political populism. Populism is a form of identity politics that combines
demagogy and opportunism with a Manichean world view
that considers society to be divided between the 'pure people'
and a 'corrupt elite' (Mudde, 2004). The 'people' form the
'heartland': a mythical and imagined place populated by a
virtuous and unified population (Taggart, 2000, p. 95). In the
United Kingdom, the 'heartland' has been defined as a mythical 'Middle England' by Powellite Conservatives or the
'native British people' by the far-right BNP. The anti-elitism
of populism is combined with an intense 'anti-pluralism' built
on the moral claim of populists to speak exclusively for 'the
people' and to depict opponents as 'enemies' of 'the people'
(Müller, 2016, p. 3). The growth of populism is reflected in
the increasing popularity of referenda as tools of direct
democracy, which are presented as authentic and direct
expressions of popular opinion. Populism is intimately related
to crisis, and feeds from a toxic combination of political
resentment, a perceived challenge to everyday life and the
presence of a charismatic leader, who can provide simple and
popular solutions to difficult and complex problems (Mudde,
2004, p. 547). Populists do not resent the establishment on
the basis of class difference, and usually do not desire a 'man
in the street' type of leader, but recognize the importance of a
remarkable, charismatic leader to solve the problems of the
'common man' according to their own values (common
sense). Populism involves the rejection of 'alien elites', and
populist leaders are often drawn from 'outsider elites' that
are connected to elites, but not part of them (Mudde, 2004,
pp. 559–560). Populism can be described as a form of 'illiberal democracy' (Zakaria, 2003) and tends to reject the

constitutional protection of minorities and the independence of state institutions such as the judiciary. The rejection of liberal democracy draws strength from the confused and often opportunistic promises of political elites. This model of populism provides a useful framework for understanding the rise and success of UKIP as a leading force in the radical right Eurosceptical populism that resulted in Brexit.

The party was formed in 1991 at the *Anti-Federalist League* by historian Alan Sked. Prior to 2010, UKIP was focused on hard Euroscepticism and, as an organization, brought together ex-Conservative Eurosceptics with fringe networks such as the *Bruges Group*. UKIP began as a 'policy-seeking', rather than a 'vote seeking', organization, and focused on the recruitment of disillusioned Conservatives to pressure the Conservative Party into adopting a harder line on Europe (Ford & Goodwin, 2014, p. 282). Between 2010 and 2016, UKIP moved from a single-issue fringe party to an effective electoral force by blending together a range of political discourses and material discontents into a populist coalition. Under the charismatic leadership of Nigel Farage, the 'Brussels-plus' strategy mobilized a significant section of the 'left behind' into a populist radical right movement. UKIP emerged at the confluence of Eurosceptic and Conservative traditions that were blended into an anti-establishment populism (Tournier-Sol, 2015). This populism fused the contradictory elements of a libertarian hyper-globalist support for Atlanticist capitalism with a Powellite 'organic patriotic Toryism' that articulated a connection between race, immigration and the British way of life (Hall, 1983, p. 38). This was achieved through the slick presentational style of UKIP leader Nigel Farage, which enabled a public school-educated and former City commodity broker to present himself as a 'plain speaking' representative of ordinary people, scourge of the Establishment and enemy of 'political correctness'. The success of Farage rested on his proven ability to translate provincial, small-minded bigotry into a media-friendly idiom (Seymour, 2015, p. 41). UKIP was led by a hyper-liberal Alanticist minority of the financial elite, but could successfully present itself as the true representative of the 'people' or 'heartland' in the struggle against corrupt, unresponsive and powerful elites, including the established parties (LibLabCon) and 'faceless' bureaucrats in Brussels.

The UKIP coalition was built on a coherent populist narrative that combined a 'hard' form of Euroscepticism, based on an opposition to the UK's membership of the EU, with a range of material and cultural concerns connected with how mainstream politicians had managed the 2008 financial crisis and EU immigration (Ford & Goodwin, 2014, p. 278). This distinction has been used to highlight the divergent class base of the UKIP coalition. In a 2012 article for the *European Journal of Political Research*, Robert Ford, Matthew J Goodwin, and David Cutts (2012, p. 224) differentiate between the mainly middle-class and Conservative-supporting 'strategic Eurosceptics' and the mainly working-class and Labour-supporting 'polite xenophobes'. They argue that the latter formed UKIP's core support and comprised 'left behind' sections of the working class from traditional Labour backgrounds; particularly older, blue collar, less-educated, white men with pessimistic outlooks. This distinction tends to overstate the importance of the working class and understate the importance of the middle class and petty bourgeoisie as the primary base of UKIP support. It also provides undue legitimation for UKIP's own self-definition as a 'working-class party' (Seymour, 2015, pp. 32–33) and reinforces a longstanding media discourse that tends to overstate the working-class origins and composition of the far-right (Rhodes, 2009, 2011). Geoffrey Evans and Jon Mellon (2016) demonstrated how the social base of the UKIP electoral coalition comprised an alliance of manual workers, employers and the self-employed, with a range of past political allegiances. Indeed, studies of voting behaviour before the 2015 general election highlighted that UKIP support was more dependent on former Conservative voters than former Labour voters and, even in working-class areas where UKIP performed well, this was often a result of the block transfer of votes from the BNP and other right-wing parties alongside the dis-engagement, disillusionment and abstention of many former Labour voters (Seymour, 2015, pp. 33–34).

Immigration was clearly a key issue mobilizing support for UKIP. The rise of the Party marked an important realignment of the far right in Britain, as the BNP and other far-right parties declined and lost support. The position of UKIP on issues of race, ethnicity and immigration and the racist *faux pas* emanating from UKIP councillors and officers, made it difficult for the Party to avoid the claim that it was the 'BNP in blazers'. The rise of UKIP can be related to long-term changes in British society and changes in the strategic priorities and policies of the mainstream political parties. The principal objective of UKIP was withdrawal from the EU and the principle motivation for a large proportion of UKIP supporters was opposition to immigration. The toxic issue of immigration and the way it could be linked with unpopular European institutions coincided with a growing disconnect between politics and significant swathes of the English population, and UKIP emerged as an electoral force with the ability to articulate and represent this disconnect (Geddes, 2014). The electoral system had produced vast regions of the United Kingdom that were taken for granted by the Labour Party and largely ignored by the Conservative Party. The Labour and Conservative parties converged around a socially liberal, pro-market consensus, and the material interests of 'left behind' groups and generationally defined views on issues such as immigration, sexual diversity and ethnic change ceased to have a mainstream expression in British politics. The Labour Party and the Liberal Democrats attempted to respond to the challenge posed by UKIP and immigration by treating immigration as a material problem linked to employment and public services, while the Conservative Party attempted to side-line UKIP as an extremist party or, in the words of David Cameron, a party of 'fruitcakes, loonies and closet racists' (Kaufmann, 2014). The Labour and Liberal Democrat approach failed to grasp the intense cultural changes generated by immigration or the intense forms of identity politics underpinning support for English nationalism and UKIP. Opposition to immigration was not just confined to areas that had directly experienced high levels of immigration, but was also present in contiguous neighbourhoods and communities (Geddes, 2014, p. 292); suggesting that immigration reflected a generalized sense of fear and anxiety in marginalized communities around the future of public services and social and cultural cohesion. Support for UKIP reflected the emergence of the kinds of 'resentful nationalism', explored in Chapter Three, that articulated material and cultural grievances and anxieties as an expression of 'national entitlement' against alien outsiders. The material concerns and cultural anxieties of the 'left behind' were manipulated by the Leave campaign, which were aligned with the interests of powerful and wealthy libertarian globalists into a coalition of support for Brexit.

'TAKE BACK CONTROL' OR 'STRONGER IN EUROPE': THE BATTLE LINES OF THE REFERENDUM CAMPAIGN

The 2015 Conservative election manifesto committed David Cameron to hold an in—out referendum on EU membership.

Cameron did not expect to win the 2015 election, and this was not, therefore, a commitment that he expected having to deliver on. The referendum was a tactical gambit designed to appease Eurosceptics within the Conservative Party and to prevent further defections and loss of support to UKIP. Following the 2015 general election, Cameron set out to negotiate a 'new deal' for the United Kingdom, and following negotiations with the other 27 EU leaders, managed to extract a range of concessions. The key issue was immigration, and the need to address the 'problem' of intra-EU migration through restricting the rights of EU migrants to social security benefits in the United Kingdom. Cameron achieved significant concessions at the February 2016 EU summit. There was an agreement that a British exemption to 'ever-closer union' could be written into EU treaties; a guarantee that non-Eurozone members would not have to fund Eurozone bailouts; and a 'red card' procedure that enabled EU legislation to be blocked by 55% of EU national parliaments. Cameron also managed some concessions around free movement and the restriction of in-work benefits. However, the negotiations failed in political terms, as Cameron did not achieve the ambitious programme of 'full-on treaty change' that he had promised. The Eurosceptic press reported the outcome of the Summit with derision: The *Daily Mail* frothed 'Call that a deal, Dave?'. The perception that the summit negotiations had failed was important, as polls showed that most of the British electorate supported remaining within a reformed EU. It also provided the context for the referendum campaign, during which David Cameron attempted unsuccessfully to make the case that the concessions were significant enough to transform him from a potential Brexit supporter to a passionate supporter of Remain. Despite the lukewarm reception to the deal, Cameron was confident of winning a referendum and decided to initiate a poll.

The campaign featured two official campaign groups. *Britain Stronger in Europe* led the Remain campaign. This was a cross-party grouping led by Will Straw (Associate Director of the left-leaning *Institute for Public Policy Research* think-tank), and it followed the strategy of successful campaigns by the Conservative Party by focusing on a small number of key messages. In this case, it was the message that EU membership underpinned the economic security of the United Kingdom, and that membership of the EU made Britain stronger and safer. The Remain campaign was supported by a formidable army of Establishment forces, including all the mainstream political parties, business organizations and interests, the TUC and most trade unions, universities and transnational organizations and interests. *VoteLeave* was the official Leave campaign group, and was led by Matthew Elliot (founder of the *Taxpayers' Alliance* — a libertarian conservative think-tank and pressure group) and Dominic Cummings (special advisor to Michael Gove). There was also *Leave.EU*, an unofficial Leave campaign founded in 2015 by Aaron Banks (businessman and UKIP funder) and Richard Tice (a property entrepreneur). Banks, or the 'man who bought Brexit', is a Bristol-based insurance magnate who donated £1 million to UKIP and £7.5 million to the *Leave.EU* campaign — arguably the largest single donation made to a political cause in British history (see Fletcher, 2016). While *VoteLeave* focused on issues of economics and political sovereignty aimed at middle-class Tories, *Leave.EU* focused doggedly on immigration in an attempt to appeal to white working-class voters in the Midlands and the North of England. On the advice of *Goddard Gunster*, a Washington-based campaign strategy firm, *Leave.EU* focused on immigration and mimicked the campaign that eventually resulted in the successful election of Donald Trump in the United States by appealing to 'emotion' rather than 'facts'. This was combined with the engagement of *Cambridge Analytica* to advise on the dark arts of 'targeted voter messaging' on social media platforms. The Leave campaigns articulated a range of simple and powerful messages. *Leave.EU* led with the slogan: 'I want my country back'. *VoteLeave* led with: 'Take back control'. The Leave campaigns put forward statements that were either misleading or factually incorrect to support their campaign — such as the claim that the United Kingdom paid £350 million a week to the EU which could be used to fund the NHS. The Leave campaigns could effectively counter an abstract and arcane Remain campaign, based on the benefits of 'pooled sovereignty' and 'transnational cooperation' within the EU and the economic threats posed by Brexit, with a populist discourse based on a rejection of political and Establishment 'experts'. The Remain and Leave campaigns became known as 'Project Fear' and 'Project Hate', respectively.

The Leave campaigns were supported, orchestrated and funded by powerful and wealthy business interests, including mega-rich hedge-fund managers. Most business interests opposed Brexit, because withdrawal from the single market would generate volatility and threaten revenues and profits. But the hedge-fund industry thrives on volatility and uncertainty, and leading figures from this sector were strong supporters of Brexit; particularly as their interests and the primacy of the City of London as a financial hub were perceived to be under threat by new EU regulations on the financial sector (Coles, 2016). Proposals included the *Alternative Investment Fund Managers Directive* (AIFMD), which set out restrictions on hedge-fund leverage and proposed new rules on depositories, remuneration, liquidity and valuation. This led many hedge-fund managers to increase their donations to the Conservative Party, and their concerns found expression in Conservative Party policies on the EU focused on deepening and liberalizing the single market and reducing 'unnecessary' regulations and bureaucracy (Coles, 2016, p. 32). Brexit exposed deep divisions in the UK's financial elites, and within the financial services sector, as large corporate banks and their CEOs largely opposed Brexit. The Leave campaigns raised £8.1 million from donors compared to £7.4 million raised by the Remain campaign. Amongst donors to *VoteLeave* were Peter Cruddas (founder of CMC Markets and worth over £1 billion), Luke Johnson of *Risk Capital Partners* and Stuart Wheeler of *IG Index*. Donors to *Leave.EU* included Aaron Banks, Richard Tice (CLS Holdings) and the campaign was partnered by *Global Britain*, which was funded by a range of entrepreneurs and asset fund managers (Coles, 2016, pp. 39–40). The Leave campaigns were also supported by a range of politicians and entrepreneurs who take a 'hyper-globalist' position regarding trade relations, and see the EU as constraining the ability of the United Kingdom to pursue bilateral trade deals with the Anglosphere and beyond.

The coalition that came together to secure Brexit, however, included a diverse range of individuals, groups and interests. To argue that 'Brexit means Brexit' obscures the diversity of interests and motivations that combined to make Brexit possible. The coalition did indeed include the oft-cited 'left behind' from the post-industrial heartlands, but equally important were libertarian hyper-globalists and 'baby-boomer Brexiters', motivated by the utopia of a de-regulated world order of free trade and free enterprise. There were also supporters of Brexit on the left who projected the notion of a 'left exit' or 'Lexit'. The case for 'Lexit' was based upon how developments around the Eurozone crisis and the EU response to the left-wing Syriza Party in Greece highlighted the undemocratic and neo-liberal nature of the EU, and the inconsistency of the left in supporting the EU, while opposing developments such as the TTIP that mirrored the regulatory form of the EU, but had a different membership composition (Tuck, 2016). These included left-wing academics and intellectuals, a section of the trade union movement including Associated Society of Locomotive Engineers and Firemen (ASLEF), Rail, Maritime and Transport Workers' Union (RMT) and the Bakers' Union, far-left political parties such as the Socialist Workers Party (SWP) and a small selection of Labour Party MPs. There were also older, Tory traditionalists, motivated by nativist and xenophobic concerns about immigration and the decline of Britain as an imperial power, and the ways that the EU threatened British sovereignty, culture and identity. These were uneasy bedfellows, but the Leave campaign was clearly orchestrated and financed by right-wing, libertarian political elites and mega-rich financial interests.

There were prominent members of the Conservative Party in both the Remain and Leave camps. The Remain campaign was backed by David Cameron, George Osborne and several leading cabinet members including Theresa May. The credibility of Cameron had been damaged by the outcome of the negotiations, and the proposed reforms did not play a significant role in the campaign. The Remain campaign was supported by a booklet sent to every household in the United Kingdom outlining the (primarily economic) rationale for remaining in the EU, and a report produced by the Treasury warning of the economic costs of Brexit. The Leave campaign included Michael Gove, Iain Duncan Smith and an opportunistic Boris Johnson. The charisma and popularity of Boris Johnson was an important factor in the campaign and the Leave side exploited the 'blue-on-blue' struggle by attacking the record of the Government on issues such as higher-rate taxation and mobilized a class discourse to undermine arguments that Brexit would harm the least well-off in society.

The Labour Party played a marginal and ambiguous role in the referendum campaign. The Remain campaign needed to mobilize Labour voters; many of whom distrusted Cameron and Osborne because of their anti-austerity policies. The tensions and contradictions that had first developed in the 1970s and 1980s around EU accession, the Bennite Euroscepticism of the AES and the SDP split came back to haunt the Party. The Labour leadership exuded indifference, and at times hostility, to the Remain campaign. Jeremy Corbyn, an established Bennite Eurosceptic, refused to share a platform with former New Labour leaders of the Labour Party or with David Cameron, and went on holiday in the middle of the campaign. Indeed, Corbyn articulated an ambiguous message on the EU, by both praising and criticizing European institutions. Consequently, faced with high levels of public mistrust and hostility on the issue of immigration, Labour Party campaigners and canvassers for Remain were unable to articulate a coherent Labour Party position on the issue, or to effectively mobilize Labour voters to support Remain.

The Leave campaigns could exploit the steep rise in net migration to the United Kingdom in 2015. An anti-immigration discourse, amplified by the right-wing tabloid media, highlighted how immigration was placing an intolerable strain on infrastructure and public services. Further increases in immigration were projected, based on the failure of the EU as a political project and the projected expansion of the EU to include Albania, Macedonia, Montenegro, Serbia and possibly Turkey (see *VoteLeave*, 2016). The Leave campaigns highlighted how the crisis in Syria and the Middle East posed a security and demographic threat to the United Kingdom. This involved an attempt to conflate migration and the refugee crisis in ways that problematized the existential future of Europe. Europe was portrayed as an aging, declining and weakened player on the global stage, surrounded by hotbeds of population growth, poverty and fanaticism (Gietel-Basten, 2016, p. 676). Populist politicians, such as Nigel Farage, also blurred EU and non-EU migration and the distinction between economic migrants and asylum seekers, and created a toxic mixture of racism and xenophobia. This was illustrated by the 'Breaking Point' poster, unveiled by Farage on the day Jo Cox was murdered, which depicted Syrian refugees entering Slovenia. The Leave campaigns were thus able to claim that Brexit was the only way to re-establish control over UK borders, and the strength of this discourse resulted in an absence of rational debate on the positive benefits of EU migration to the UK economy and public services.

The issues of immigration and the economy dominated media coverage of the campaign, and the campaign became increasingly polarized as a simple choice between the economy and immigration, combined with a focus on distrust in government and the Establishment (Hobolt, 2016, p. 1263). The linkages between print, television and social media were exploited particularly effectively by the Leave campaigns (Seaton, 2016). The print media were preponderantly pro-leave. *The Sun*, *Daily Mail* and *Daily Express* provided particularly ardent and vitriolic support for the Leave campaign. The pro-Leave tabloid media tended to blur fact and ideology, in an anti-EU agenda driven by the interests of proprietors and editors, and produced the slogans, voice and (largely false) prospectus of the Leave campaign: a catalogue of distortions, half-truths and downright lies (Barnett, 2016). While the BBC, and other public service broadcasters, had a responsibility to be 'balanced', the ways in which balance was operationalized allowed the print media to set the agenda and frame the debate. In the coverage of the debate, issues were treated in a Manichean way and evidence and expertise on each side of the debate were merely assigned rather than explored and interrogated proportionately. There was additional pressure on the BBC because pro-Brexit voices tended to be anti-BBC. The EU referendum campaign also highlighted how social media acts as a self-reinforcing 'echo chamber' that polarizes debate and opinion and encourages extremist and inflammatory language and arguments. The community and the message tend to merge in online worlds, and the binary and Manichean nature of the referendum was particularly vulnerable to the polarizing potential of social media, which tended to recast the limits of 'acceptable' opinion and 'normalize' extremism (Seaton, 2016, p. 336). The Leave campaigns were to ultimately prevail, when, following four decades of uneasy and increasingly fractious relations between the United Kingdom and the EU, the British people voted narrowly in favour of leaving the EU. But who were the main support base for Brexit? Was it really a working-class revolt?

BREAKING AWAY! THE MYTH OF THE NORTHERN WORKING-CLASS REVOLT

The referendum decision for the United Kingdom to exit the EU by a narrow margin of 51.9–48.1% with a 72.2% turnout was not expected by either the Leave or Remain campaigns (see Swales, 2016, for a detailed breakdown of the results). The Leave campaign did not expect to win and produced no clear blueprint of what Brexit would look like in practice. The decision evoked panic within global markets, as the pound sank to a thirty-one year low against the US dollar, and $2 trillion was wiped from the value of shares at a global level. The decision also evoked an immediate political crisis in the United Kingdom, as Prime Minister David Cameron resigned and the Labour Party was plunged into a damaging internal leadership battle. The voting patterns in the referendum demonstrated an important set of divisions and cleavages in British society based on geography, education, income and age (Goodwin & Heath, 2016). The results were compiled by local authority area and a clear majority of areas voted to Leave. There was a stark contrast between Scotland, where all areas voted Remain, and England, where every region except London voted to Leave. The vote in Wales did not deviate from the national trend (52.2% leave compared to 47.5% remain), and in Northern Ireland, a majority voted Remain (55.8%). The Leave vote was higher than expected in the East Midlands, West Midlands, East Coast regions of England, the Welsh valleys and parts of South West and North West England; although it was lower than expected in the cities of Birmingham, Leicester and Nottingham. This was repeated in other urban city areas such as Oxford, Cambridge, Bristol, Cardiff, York, Norwich, Sheffield, Warwick, Winchester and Swansea. While London voted to Remain, there were several boroughs, mainly on the Essex and Kent borders, where Leave did better than expected. The most important predictors of these geographical variations were the proportion of 60−64 year olds in the population, the proportion of the population in lower supervisory and technical occupations, the proportion of the population born outside the United Kingdom but in the EU and the size of the Pakistani community (Harris & Charlton, 2016).

The relationship between immigration, race and ethnicity and the Leave vote was complex (Harris & Charlton, 2016, pp. 2124−2125). In some pro-Leave areas, such as South Staffordshire (76% Leave), only 1% of the population were migrants from the EU, and in the 20 areas in the United Kingdom with the lowest levels of EU migration, 15 voted Leave. Evidence suggests that support for Brexit was related to the rate of change in EU migration, rather than absolute levels of migration, and areas such as Redditch and Lincoln, which had seen a rapid increase in the rate of migration, there was a strong vote for Leave. Immigration was a factor in less ethnically-mixed areas with high seasonal immigration from the EU, such as East Anglia, but not in ethnically diverse urban areas in large towns and cities. While most British Asians voted to remain in the EU (68−32%), a significant minority of nearly one-third voted for Brexit and supported a campaign that was explicitly racist and xenophobic. Recent research by the Runnymede Trust (Khan & Weekes-Bernard, 2016) has highlighted the ambivalence of Black, Asian and Minority Ethnic (BAME) communities towards the EU; including a lower proclivity to identify as 'European' or to pursue 'free movement' within the EU. The transnational networks populated by British Asians tend to bypass Europe and embrace country of origin, diaspora and Commonwealth. Negative orientations to the EU could also have been the product of resentment based on the contrast between the easy assimilation of mainly white migrants from Eastern Europe with the racism and prejudice faced by British Asians, and the contrast between the free access of EU migrants to the United Kingdom compared to the restrictions and barriers faced by migrants from the Asian sub-continent (Ehsan, 2017; Parveen, 2016). The latter point was a prominent refrain of leading British Asian Leave supporters, such as Government minister Priti Patel, while campaigning for Brexit in Asian communities (Chandhoke, 2016).

A close analysis of the results of the referendum destroys the convenient myth, put forward by cosmopolitan liberal supporters of Remain, that Brexit was primarily caused by the support of the 'white working class' in marginalized rust-belt communities of the 'North'. This is not to deny that many individuals within these communities supported Leave, and, of course, many did for the reasons explored in Chapter Three. The key point is that this was not the crucial group of voters that delivered Brexit. The key base of support for Brexit can be found amongst older, less-educated, Conservative-supporting, *Daily Mail/Daily Express*-reading, middle-class voters in the South of England that tended towards authoritarian, nativist and xenophobic values and attitudes. This was highlighted in the divisions exposed by the Brexit vote. The Leave vote was highest in areas where average levels of schooling were low. In terms of occupation, most professional workers voted Remain, while high/low median hourly pay provided a good indicator for support for Remain and Leave, respectively. There was also a clear generational division. The Leave vote was higher in areas where a large proportion of the population was over 65 and lower where the population was younger. A popular view is that the outcome of the referendum was decided by working-class voters in the North of England. However, considering differential levels of turnout and the size of the denominator population, the majority of Leave voters lived in the South of England, and 59% of Leave voters were middle class (A, B or C1) compared to 41% who were working class (C2, D or E). Middle-class Leave voters were crucial to the final vote because the middle class constituted two-thirds of those voting (Hennig & Dorling, 2016, p. 20). There was a clear relationship between support for Brexit and pre-referendum attitudes and voting behaviour, including a strong correlation between support for Brexit and support for UKIP (96%) and the Conservative Party (58%), and support for Remain with support for the Labour Party (63%), SNP (64%), Liberal Democrats (70%) and Green Party (75%) (Lord Ashcroft Polls, 2016). The data also showed an interesting relationship between support for Brexit and perceptions of national identity. Support for Leave was 79% amongst individuals that defined themselves as 'English', compared to 60% support for Remain amongst individuals that defined themselves as

British. There was a strong correlation between support for Brexit and individuals with negative attitudes to multiculturalism, globalization and environmentalism, which highlighted the relationship between support for Brexit and authoritarian attitudes and values (Kaufmann, 2016).

SUMMARY AND CONCLUSION

Brexit is part of a broader wave of populism that has been generated by the disruptive effects of the 2008 financial crisis and long-term legitimation crisis of party political systems of democratic representation. In the United Kingdom, this combined with the post-imperial crisis of the British state and the financialized trajectory of the British economy to produce a particularly potent form of Eurosceptic popular nationalism that articulated the material and cultural anxieties and concerns of 'left behind' segments of the British population, but which was led and orchestrated by an outsider faction of the financial elite. New Labour attempted to de-politicize the 'Europe question' as part of a 'passive revolution' that attempted to replace democratic contestation with technocratic governance. The 2010–2015 Coalition government led by David Cameron continued with the technocratic centrist approach to governance, but pursued an austerity programme that generated social and political polarization, insecurity and anxiety alongside an increasingly belligerent Eurosceptic rhetoric. The contradictions of this approach opened a political space on the right of British politics, and UKIP shifted from a marginal single-issue party to a potent populist movement led by the charismatic Nigel Farage. UKIP combined the Atlanticist phantasies of a faction of the financial and political elites with the 'resentful nationalism' of 'left behind'. The 'left behind' that were mobilized were wider than the working class in the de-industrialized North and, indeed, the middle class and petty bourgeoisie in the South of England were the most important part of the coalition mobilized by UKIP and the Leave campaigns in favour of Brexit.

CHAPTER FIVE

POST-BREXIT TRAJECTORIES

The main legacy of the EU referendum is turmoil, disruption and unpredictability. Brexit seems to mark a historical moment where the normal rules of politics have been discontinued and we exist in a state of suspended disbelief with long-term forces appearing on the horizon (Guldi, 2017, p. 152). The 'Europe question' continues to tear apart the Conservative Party and, notwithstanding unexpected signs of revival in the 2017 general election, threatens the long-term unity and viability of the Labour Party. UKIP now appears as an ephemeral beast, which emerged from nowhere to deliver Brexit, only to immediately expire post-Brexit as its *raison d'être* disappeared and the tensions between its libertarian leadership and nativist support base erupted into toxic internecine conflict and organizational implosion. Does this mean that the grievances, anxieties and concerns articulated by UKIP and harnessed by the Leave campaign have been resolved? In the year following the referendum, the 'Brexit means Brexit' dictum has become even less plausible and convincing. Was Brexit really a proxy vote for a range of more fundamental issues and grievances, and if so, does the Brexit vote address these or threaten to intensify the tensions and contradictions that generated them in the first place? The libertarian champions of Brexit tend to see the decision to leave the EU as the ultimate stride into the free market utopia of Thatcherism, with the bonus of huge patriotic symbolism (Harris, 2017). In the world of Brexiteer MPs David Davis and Liam Fox, a low-tax, low-regulation 'Singapore-on-Thames' will thrive without the fetters of EU regulations. The 2017 election, however, seems to have quashed these dreams, along with the model of unfettered neo-liberal capitalism on which it depends.

The popular 'counter-transformation' that underpinned support for UKIP and the Leave campaign attacked the consensus and power bloc that had developed around cosmopolitan social liberalism and finance-led neo-liberalism from the right (Seymour, 2015, p. 37). The populist surge that has erupted around the world since the 2008 financial crisis articulates a deep disenchantment with neo-liberalism, and a rejection of an economic model based on globalized free trade, liberalized financial markets, privatization, deregulation and low levels of taxation (Beckett, 2017). The architecture of neo-liberalism was dented by the 2008 financial crisis and highlighted the unviability of free market capitalism (Crouch, 2011; Gamble, 2009; Krippner, 2012). Decades of neo-liberal dogma on the virtues of the minimal state were demolished by a state-led rescue of neo-liberalism through bank bail-outs and quantitative easing. The financialized model of capitalism was no longer delivering economic growth, but rather wage stagnation, employment precarity, declining pensions and austerity were undermining the economic security and personal well-being of individuals. This contrasted with the situation of economic and political elites, who were seen as responsible for the financial crisis, but had not suffered personally from its after-effects, resulting in increasing levels of public anger and concern over the excessive pay of 'fat cat' company executives and the sleazy and corrupt behaviour of politicians.

The waves of political populism that emerged following the 2008 crisis articulated these concerns, and the events of 2016 and 2017 marked the apogee of the political crisis of neo-liberalism, with Brexit in the United Kingdom and the election of Donald Trump in the United States. The crisis of neo-liberalism defines the economic, cultural and political trajectories beyond Brexit and are defined by three interrelated developments. First, a dogmatic belief in the benefits of financialized neo-liberal capitalism has dominated mainstream British politics since the 1980s, including the 'state projects' of Thatcherism and New Labour and extending across smaller parties such as the Liberal Democrats and the SNP in Scotland. Brexit inflicted a serious, and perhaps fatal, blow against the foundations of this dogma and has forced a re-engagement with models of 'organized capitalism' that have been considered heretical since the 1980s. This highlights the emergence of a 'double movement' against 'market fundamentalism' as predicted by Karl Polanyi (2001). Second, the populist forces associated with Brexit assaulted the neo-liberal consensus from the right, and this produced a considerable level of ethnic, racial and inter-cultural tension and hatred encouraged by the right-wing popular press. The resulting radical right political discourse emboldened the open and public expression of intolerant views and opinions, and scarred community and inter-community relations. In the context of insults, threats and intimidation, many EU migrants are leaving or are planning to leave the United Kingdom. Third, there has been a de-alignment between the main political parties and the cleavages and divisions that have emerged and developed around Brexit; which, as the 2017 general election demonstrated, has become the most

significant issue in contemporary British politics. The
Conservative Party is a coalition of nationalists who voted
Leave and business interests who voted to Remain. The
Labour Party is a coalition of urban liberals who voted
Remain and the white working class who voted Leave
(Lanchester, 2016). Both parties are now unstable coalitions,
and this suggests that politics will become increasingly turbu-
lent and unpredictable in the post-Brexit era. I will explore
each of these developments in more detail and conclude with
an exploration of the global implications of Brexit.

ECONOMIC TRAJECTORIES

The economic insecurities that motivated support for Brexit
were a reaction against the market fundamentalism that has
underpinned the financialized trajectory of the British economy for decades, and articulated demands for greater control
and regulation of the globalized economy. A gap has emerged
between the anti-neo-liberal rhetoric of the May government
and the neo-liberal rationale underpinning the Brexit negotiations. This has focused on post-Brexit trade relations and
trading partners, rather than the issue of how to construct an
economy that addresses the inequalities and discontents that
underpinned support for Brexit. The negotiations are underpinned by the logic of free market competition and the need
to attract multinational and transnational capital to the
United Kingdom. Leading supporters of Brexit see the logical
policy corollary of this as a post-Brexit UK marked by low
levels of corporation tax, investment subsidies, light-touch
regulation and flexible labour markets. This is likely to
increase inequality, further polarize wealth and dilute existing
democratic controls over the corporate sector (Morgan,
2017, p. 122). The negotiations between the United Kingdom

and EU on these issues have made virtually no progress, as both sides are unwilling to compromise on the relationship between access to the single market and the free movement of labour. There are also enduring divisions within the economic and political elites over the post-Brexit trajectory of the British economy. Business interests such as the Confederation of British Industry (CBI) and the Institute of Directors have warned the Government against the dangers of a 'cliff edge' Brexit, and this is overlain by tensions between libertarians and conservatives in the Conservative Party. The attempt to recognize and respond to the concerns of nativist and 'left behind' conservatives while delivering a 'hard' but 'business-friendly' Brexit, has paralyzed the Conservative governments led by Theresa May. In the context of the uncertainty created by Brexit, and the ongoing division in the political and economic elites, it is unclear how a stable and viable accumulation strategy held together by a strong and stable 'hegemonic bloc' can emerge on the political right in post-Brexit Britain.

Indeed, current trends point towards deeper uncertainty and instability leading to low growth rates and a declining tax base. This is likely to intensify rather than ameliorate the long-term structural problems of the British economy, and leave the socio-economic grievances that fuelled Brexit unresolved. The British economy continues to be out-performed by the Eurozone economies and indicators such as a decline in the sale of new cars highlights low levels of consumer confidence. Banks are planning or threatening to move away from London to Amsterdam, Frankfurt and Dublin, which is threatening the financial pre-eminence of the City and its role as 'investment banker for Europe' (Elliot & Treanor, 2017). The return of EU migrants following Brexit also threatens the long-term viability of important sectors of the British economy. There was a 36% increase in the number of EU migrants returning home in the year following Brexit, which threatens sectors such as agriculture, food processing and hospitality and the long-term sustainability of social care and the NHS (Doward & Robertson, 2017). The return of EU labour, along with the weak pound and the possible imposition of tariffs on food, impacts on every aspect of the UK's food chain and threatens the nutritional health of the nation (Rayner, 2017). Brexit threatens the rights and protections that EU membership offered British workers (TUC, 2016a, 2016b) and it is unclear if Theresa May's pro-worker rhetoric will prevent a 'bonfire of regulations' that will further undermine the economic security and health and safety of British workers (Gumbrell-McCormick & Hyman, 2017, p. 178). If the forecasts for lower growth following Brexit prove to be correct, this is likely to generate further austerity including reduced welfare benefits and state investment. The economic dislocations associated with Brexit are likely to generate a monetary policy based on zero-bound interest rates that will constrain savings and undermine the long-term viability of pension schemes. Current economic trends and trajectories suggest that Brexit is most likely to hurt those groups in society who were most likely to support Brexit: the retired, the just-about to retire and those most dependent on the state (Morgan, 2017, p. 123)

SOCIAL AND CULTURAL TRAJECTORIES

Brexit was underpinned by the emergence of an increasingly politicized form of English nationalism. This reflected a combination of material grievances and anxieties generated by de-industrialization, the 2008 financial crisis and state-led austerity and a set of cultural grievances and anxieties generated by increasing levels of EU immigration and an opposition to multiculturalism and cosmopolitan social liberalism.

The central significance of EU immigration to the concerns and anxieties of the 'left behind' and the elite status of the EU allowed a 'resentful' English nationalism to dovetail with the politics of the EU led by a hyper-liberal and globalist faction of the political and economic elite. The referendum campaign highlighted the existence of an ongoing 'culture war' in British society between libertarian cosmopolitans and conservative nativists. The populist forces associated with Brexit assaulted the neo-liberal consensus from the right. This produced a considerable level of ethnic, racial and inter-cultural tension and hatred, and the radical right political discourse emboldened the open and public expression of intolerant views and opinions. The referendum resulted in the release of vitriol and hatred on both sides of the debate, as Remain supporters were dubbed as 'unpatriotic traitors' by Leave supporters and the latter labelled as 'backward', 'xenophobic' and 'racist' by their opponents. The opposing sides in the culture war did not, however, map neatly onto the opposing sides of the EU referendum debate, as the Leave campaign was funded, organized and led by libertarians with a cosmopolitan interest in global free trade. The electoral success of UKIP and the Leave campaigns was based on how the question of EU membership was used to frame the post-liberal concerns of the 'left behind', and this encouraged and legitimated the forms of public and 'celebratory' racism that have emerged since the referendum. In the short term, the legacy of Brexit is likely to be the emboldening of nativist, post-liberal groups and interests in British society and legitimation of racial and ethnic intolerance, discrimination and violence. The potency of this threat is likely to increase if the economic concerns and anxieties of Leave supporters are not addressed by a viable post-Brexit accumulation strategy. The threat could of course recede, if a viable programme of economic reform combined with a commitment to cosmopolitan values were to develop on the left; an increasingly realistic proposition following the 2017 general election performance of the Corbyn-led Labour Party.

However, the legacy of a Brexit from the right remains the dominant socio-cultural dynamic in post-Brexit British society. Immediately following the referendum, there was a spike in hate crimes against migrants and ethnic minorities. This is part of a more generalized intolerance that is fed and nurtured by the right-wing popular press. The *Daily Mail* and *Daily Express* have continued to stoke intolerance and hatred since the referendum, with a particular focus on the unpatriotic and treacherous status of anyone who dares to defy the will of 'the people' for a 'hard' and permanent Brexit, including Establishment institutions such as the judiciary and the BBC. Intense levels of hatred and vitriol continue to reverberate around the social media firmament, with death and rape threats issued against prominent Remain supporters. This enmity continues to be reciprocated by prominent Remain supporters, who continue to highlight the 'stupidity' of Brexit, and the 'backward', 'racist' and 'xenophobic' nature of Leave supporters. The culture war continues after the vote to Brexit, and impacts on the everyday lives of EU migrants. Many are leaving or planning to leave the United Kingdom because of insults, threats and intimidation, and individuals are being forced to re-assesses their sense of belonging in a post-Brexit climate dominated by virulent forms of English ethno-nationalism. There is evidence of EU migrants, many of whom perform vital work in the NHS and other important sectors, planning or preparing to return to their country of origin after being subject to ethnic abuse, or because they no longer feel comfortable in the febrile post-Brexit environment. The decisions to leave are driven by emotion, frustration, sorrow, anger and feelings of betrayal. Many have lived in the United Kingdom for decades, have British partners and children, but no longer feel secure or wanted because of threats and intimidation. There have been reports of broken windows and children of EU workers being told to 'go home' by fellow pupils at school (Henley, 2017). In 2016, 117,000 EU nationals left the United Kingdom, marking a 36% increase on 2015 levels (ONS, 2017). Other research suggests that 47% of highly skilled EU workers in the United Kingdom are considering leaving over the next five years (Deloitte, 2017). The precarious status of EU migrants is compounded by a series of unresolved issues concerning the social rights of the 3.5 million EU migrants living in the United Kingdom, which include rights to residency, education, work, social security and health (Henley, 2017). The current plans to introduce a 'settled status' register, ID cards and minimum income thresholds highlights the real possibility of 'tiered citizenship' in post-Brexit Britain, with EU migrants being reduced to 'second class' citizens (Travis, 2017).

POLITICAL TRAJECTORIES

The 'Europe question' has dominated post-war British politics and generated fundamental divisions within both the Conservative Party and the Labour Party. The state projects of Thatcherism and New Labour attempted, in different ways, to maintain the active consent of British society to the ongoing financialization of the British economy. New Labour developed into a technocratic form of governance that embraced economic and social liberalism, and severed the institutional and cultural linkages between the Party and the British working class. The 'modernization' of the Conservative Party under the leadership of David Cameron was an attempt to abandon the 'Nasty Party' image of the Thatcher and

Major eras through an agenda of social and economic liberalism and a more cooperative relationship with the EU. This tended to marginalize the Powellite, middle-class support base of the Party. These processes of de-alignment within the two main parties left nativist, middle-class conservatives and the marginalized and socially conservative sections of the working class without a political home, and produced fertile ground for the emergence of UKIP and the building of a support base for Brexit. This process of de-alignment has defined the political disruption and turbulence since the referendum. Brexit was both responsible for the 2017 general election and emerged as the most important single issue in the election. The significance of the 2017 general election was that it highlighted how Brexit had transformed the political agendas of both mainstream parties towards a rejection of neo-liberalism. The Conservative manifesto rejected the 'cult of selfish individualism' and 'untrammelled free markets' and highlighted the need for regulation to ensure 'the correct ordering of the economy' and to 'protect and enhance the rights of workers'. The Labour Party manifesto promised an 'economy that works for all', and put forward policies on nationalization, enhanced trade union rights, restrictions on the City of London and the introduction of an 'industrial strategy' to modernize the economy (Beckett, 2017).

One way of interpreting the 2017 election results is that party support reflected the two sides of the referendum result: the Conservatives attracted 60% of the leave vote and more than half of UKIP's support from the 2015 election including voters who supported restrictions on immigration, while the Labour Party was widely perceived as the party of 'soft Brexit' and included voters who supported maintaining access to the European single market (Walker, 2017). However, the prospect of a 'nuclear winter' in which Labour was wiped-out in its Brexit-supporting industrial heartlands failed to materialize — except in the outlier cases of Mansfield and North East Derbyshire. The election seemed to kill off the mythical *Homo Brexitus* (Edgar, 2017), whose nativism and antipathy of social liberalism was predicted to bury the Labour Party under an avalanche of virulent ethno-nationalist identity politics (see Denham & Kenny, 2016). The agenda of state-led regeneration and an end to austerity not only energized young people into an engagement with electoral politics (Birch, 2016), but also attracted many Leave voters in Brexit strongholds such as Birmingham and Coventry with an agenda replete with social liberal references and policies — including support for immigration. This suggests that social liberal values are more prevalent than the outcome of the referendum suggested, and that some of the opposition to immigration in the Brexit vote reflected individuals making a logical assessment of their position in the political economy of Britain, rather than xenophobia and an inability to understand complex economic arguments (Gough, 2017).

Despite the relative success of the 2017 election campaign, the post-Brexit Labour Party remains unstable and its social base wrought with tensions and contradictions. The Party leadership of Jeremy Corbyn, John McDonnell and Diane Abbott was never part of the New Labour power bloc or the neo-liberal consensus, but vestiges of a pre-New Labour left forged in the Bennite battles around the AES in the late 1970s and the early 1980s. This explains the ambivalence of the Party leadership towards Brexit and the division between the predominantly 'New Labour' MPs in Parliament and the Corbynite membership mobilized by groups such as *Momentum*. The Conservative Party is also paralyzed by internal tensions and contradictions, which finds expression in the interminable struggle between an expanding variety of Brexits: 'hard Brexit', 'dirty Brexit', 'clean Brexit', 'soft Brexit', 'dog's Brexit' 'cliff edge Brexit', 'red, white and blue Brexit', 'smooth Brexit', 'business-friendly Brexit', 'smart Brexit', 'have-your-cake-and-eat-it Brexit', 'Schrödinger's Brexit' — the list expands almost daily. This poses a significant problem for the Conservative Party as it is forced to balance the pressure for a 'hard' Brexit from the libertarian globalist right, pressure for social and economic intervention from the nativist and former-UKIP right and pressure for a 'business-friendly' Brexit from technocratic business interests. UKIP does not seem to have a life beyond Brexit. The objective of leaving the EU has been achieved, and the established parties are beginning to address the concerns of the 'left behind' at least at a rhetorical level. Perhaps this is the ultimate proof that Brexit really does mean more than Brexit.

GLOBAL TRAJECTORIES

The sentiments that led to Brexit are not exclusive to Britain, and populist parties and movements have developed across Europe on both the populist right and the populist left (Hobolt, 2016, p. 1260; Kriesi et al., 2012), including the *Front National* (FN) in France and the *Partij voor de Vrijheid* (PVV) in the Netherlands, *Freiheitliche Partei Österreichs* (FPÖ) in Austria on the right and Podemos in Spain and SYRIZA in Greece on the left. Radical right populist parties currently form the ruling party in several EU nation states in Central and Eastern Europe, including the *Law and Justice Party* in Poland and the *Fidesz Party* in Hungary. These developments are clearly linked to the same dynamics that produced Brexit: the economic contradictions and the political crisis of neo-liberal globalism following the 2008 financial crisis. In the aftermath of the Brexit referendum, many European elites were concerned about Brexit having a contagion effect across the EU. The leaders of radical right Eurosceptic parties reacted with jubilation to the Brexit decision. Marine Le Pen, Leader of the French FN, proclaimed that the result was a 'victory for freedom', and called for an immediate referendum in France and a French exit (Frexit) from the EU. Geert Wilders, leader of the Dutch PVV, declared that, following Brexit, the 'EU is more or less dead', and also called for an immediate referendum in the Netherlands and a 'Nexit'. Despite this initial hubris, the level of EU support started to increase following Brexit and the Eurosceptic populist right have suffered defeats in Austria, the Netherlands, France, Italy and Finland. However, it is currently unclear whether this reflects a public endorsement of the new 'roadmap' of EU development carved out by the emerging Merkel-Macron leadership axis or fear of the possible catastrophic effects of EU exit, highlighted by the example of a semi-detached EU member state such as the United Kingdom attempting to extricate itself from decades of European integration (cf. Kundnani, 2017; Nougayrède, 2017). There are clear parallels between Brexit and the election of Donald Trump in the United States. Trump declared his support for Brexit declaring that it was a 'great thing' and reflected the anger of ordinary people to immigration and foreign competition: 'They are angry over borders, they are angry over people coming into the country and taking over and nobody even noticing. They are angry about many, many things'. The relative success of Bernie Sanders in the Democratic Primary, however, highlights how hope can also emerge from the rubble of collapsed neo-liberal certainties. Brexit is part of a fundamental reordering of the world following the 2008 crisis: only time will tell if the 'double movement' reflex against free market neo-liberalism takes a progressive or regressive route.

BIBLIOGRAPHY

Aaronovitch, S. (1981). *The road from Thatcherism: The alternative economic strategy*. London: Lawrence and Wishart.

Aglietta, M. (1979). *A theory of capitalist regulation*. London: New Left Books.

Albrow, M. (1996). *The global age: State and society beyond modernity*. Cambridge: Polity.

Anderson, B. (2006). *Imagined communities: Reflections on the origins and spread of nationalism*. London: Verso.

Antonucci, L., Horvath, L., Kutiyski, Y., & Krouwel, A. (2017). The malaise of the squeezed middle: Challenging the narrative of the "left behind" Brexiter'. *Competition and Change*, *21*(3), 211–229.

Ashcroft, R., & Bevir, M. (2016). Pluralism, national identity and citizenship: Britain after Brexit. *The Political Quarterly*, *87*(3), 355–359.

Bachmann, V., & Sidaway, J. D. (2016). Brexit geopolitics. *Geoforum*, *77*, 47–50.

Baker, D., Gamble, A., & Ludlam, S. (1993). 1846... 1906... 1996? Conservative splits and European integration. *The Political Quarterly*, *64*(4), 415–442.

Baker, D., Gamble, A., & Seawright, D. (2002). Sovereign nations and global markets: Modern British conservatism and hyperglobalism. *The British Journal of Politics & International Relations*, 4(3), 399–428.

Barnett, S. (2016). The tragic downfall of British media: How did the country that produced the BBC and the Economist fail so spectacularly at journalism in the lead up to Brexit? *Foreign Policy*, July 8.

Bauman, Z. (1991). *Modernity and ambivalence*. Cambridge: Polity.

Bauman, Z. (2004). *Europe: An unfinished adventure*. Cambridge: Polity.

Bechhofer, F., & McCrone, D. (2009). 'National identity, nationalism and constitutional change'. In F. Bechhofer & D. McCrone (Eds.), *National identity, nationalism and constitutional change* (pp. 1–16). Basingstoke: Palgrave Macmillan.

Beck, G. (2010). *The Overton window*. New York, NY: Threshold Editions.

Beck, U. (2000). *What is globalization?* Cambridge: Polity.

Beckett, A. (2017). How Britain fell out of love with the free market. *The Guardian*, August 5.

Bieler, A. (2006). *The struggle for a social Europe: Trade unions and EMU in times of global restructuring*. Manchester: Manchester University Press.

Birch, S. (2016). Our new voters: Brexit, political mobilization and the emerging electoral cleavage. *Juncture*, 23(2), 107–110.

Bonefeld, W. (2002). European integration: The market, the political and class. *Capital and Class*, 26(2), 117–142.

Bonefeld, W., & Burnham, P. (1998). The politics of counter inflationary credibility in Britain, 1990-94. *Review of Radical Political Economics*, 30(1), 32–52.

Buckler, S., & Dolowitz, D. P. (2004). Can fair be efficient? New Labour, social liberalism and British economic policy. *New Political Economy*, 9(1), 23–38.

Callaghan, J. (2007). Pivotal powers: The British Labour Party and European unity since 1945. *Capital and Class*, 93(Autumn), 199–215.

Carchedi, G. (2001). *For another Europe: A class analysis of European economic integration*. London: Verso.

Castells, M. (1997). *The information age: Economy, society and culture. Volume two: The power of identity*. Oxford: Blackwell.

Castells, M. (2000b). *The information age: Economy, society and culture. Volume three: The end of millennium*. Oxford: Blackwell.

Chakrabortty, A. (2016). After a campaign scarred by bigotry, it's become OK to be racist in Britain. *The Guardian*, June 28.

Chandhoke, H. (2016). Brexit: Did British-Asians just put a xenophobic gun to their heads. *International Business Times*. Retrieved from http://www.ibtimes.co.uk/brexit-did-british-asians-just-put-xenophobic-gun-their-heads-1567424. Accessed on July 11, 2017.

Chang, H. (2010). *23 things they didn't tell you about capitalism*. London: Allen Lane.

Clarke, S. (1988). *Keynesianism, monetarism and the crisis of the state*. Aldershot: Edward Elgar.

Coates, D. (1995). 'UK underperformance: Claim and reality'. In D. Coates & J. Hillard (Eds.), *UK economic decline: Key texts* (pp. 3–24). London: Prentice Hall.

Coleman, D. (2016). A demographic rationale for Brexit. *Population and Development Review*, 42(4), 681–692.

Coles, T. J. (2016). *The great Brexit swindle: Why the mega-rich and free market fanatics conspired to force Britain from the European Union*. West Hoathly: Clairview Books.

Condor, F., & Fenton, S. (2012). Thinking across domains: Class, nation and racism in England and Britain. *Ethnicities*, 12(4), 385–393.

Conquest, R. (1999). *Reflections on a ravaged century*. London: W.W. Norton and Company.

Conservative Party. (2010). *Invitation to join the government of Britain: The Conservative manifesto 2010*. London: Conservative Party.

Crewe, I., & King, A. (1995). *SDP: The birth, life and death of the Social Democratic Party*. Oxford: Oxford University Press.

Crouch, C. (2011). *The strange non-death of neoliberalism*. Cambridge: Polity.

Curtice, J. (2016). Brexit: Behind the referendum. *Political Insight*, 7(2), 4–7.

Curtis, P. (2010). Gordon Brown calls Labour supporter a "bigoted woman". *The Guardian*, April 28.

Daddow, O. (2012). The UK media and "Europe": From permissive consensus to destructive dissent. *International Affairs, 88*(6), 1219–1236.

Davis, A., & Walsh, C. (2015). The role of the state in the financialization of the UK economy. *Political Studies, 64*(3), 666–682.

Deighton, A. (1993). Britain and the Cold War 1945-55: An overview. In B. Brivati & H. Jones (Eds.), *From reconstruction to integration: Britain and Europe since 1945* (pp. 7–17). Leicester: Leicester University Press.

Deloitte. (2017). *Power up: The UK workplace*. London: Deloitte.

Denham, J., & Kenny, M. (2016). Labour and the national question after Brexit. *Renewal, 24*(4), 28–31.

De Vries, C. E., & Edwards, E. (2009). Taking Europe to its extremes: Extremist parties and public Euroscepticism. *Party Politics, 15*(1), 5–28.

Dodd, P. (1986). 'Englishness and the National Culture'. In R. Colls & P. Dodd (Eds.), *Englishness, politics and culture 1888–1920* (pp. 1–28). London: Croom Helm.

Doward, J., & Robertson, H. (Eds.). (2017). From translators and fruit pickers to hotel workers – Key EU migrants we rely on to keep the economy going. *The Observer*, July 30.

Dyson, K. (2000). Europeanization, Whitehall culture and the Treasury as institutional veto player: A constructivist approach to economic and monetary union. *Public Administration, 78*(4), 897–914.

Edgar, D. (2017). We thought Homo Brexitus was the future, but he isn't winning anymore. *The Guardian*, June 28.

Ehsan, R. (2017). Inside the British Asian Brexit vote – And why it contains a few surprises. *The Conversation*. Retrieved from http://theconversation.com/inside-the-british-asian-brexit-vote-and-why-it-contains-a-few-surprises-72931. Accessed July 11, 2017.

Elliot, L., & Treanor, J. (2017). Financial sector could double within 25 years, predicts Bank governor. *The Guardian*, August 4.

Eurofound (2016). *European jobs monitor Annual Report 2016*. Dublin: Eurofound.

European Commission. (2012). European citizenship: Report. *Standard Eurobarometer*, 77. Retrieved from http://ec.europa.eu/commfrontoffice/publicopinion/archives/eb/eb77/eb77_citizen_en.pdf. Accessed on July 20, 2017.

Evans, G., & Mellon, J. (2016). Working-class votes and conservative losses: Solving the UKIP puzzle. *Parliamentary Affairs*, 69, 464–479.

Featherstone, K. (1988). *Socialist parties and European integration: A comparative history*. Manchester: Manchester University Press.

Fekete, L. (2016). Flying the flag for neo-liberalism. *Race and Class*, 58(3), 3–22.

Fenton, S. (2012). Resentment, class and social sentiments about the nations: The ethnic majority in England. *Ethnicities*, 12(4), 465–483.

Fletcher, M. (2016). Aaron Banks: The man who bought Brexit. *New Statesman*, October 16.

Fontana, C., & Parsons, C. (2015). 'One woman's prejudice': Did Margaret Thatcher cause Britain's anti-Europeanism? *Journal of Common Market Studies*, 53(1), 89–105.

Ford, R., & Goodwin, M. J. (2014). Understanding UKIP: Identity, social change and the left behind. *The Political Quarterly*, *85*(3), 277–284.

Ford, R., Goodwin, M. J., & Cutts, D. (2012). Strategic Eurosceptics and polite xenophobes: Support for the United Kingdom Independence Party (UKIP) in the 2009 European parliament elections. *European Journal of Political Research*, *51*(2), 204–234.

Ford, R., & Somerville, W. (2010). Immigration and the 2010 election: More than meets the eye. In T. Finch & D. Goodhart (Eds.), *Immigration under labour* (pp. 10–14). London: IPPR.

Forster, A. (2002). *Euroscepticism in contemporary British politics: Opposition to Europe in the British Conservative and Labour Parties since 1945*. London: Routledge.

Foster, J. B., & Magdoff, F. (2009). *The great financial crisis: Causes and consequences*. New York, NY: Monthly Review Press.

Franklin, M., Marsh, M., & McLaren, L. (1994). Uncorking the bottle: Popular opposition to European unification in the wake of Maastricht. *Journal of Common Market Studies*, *32*(4), 455–472.

Franklin, M., Van der Eijk, C., & Marsh, M. (1995). Referendum outcomes and trust in government: Public support for Europe in the wake of Maastricht. *West European Politics*, *18*(3), 101–117.

Freedman, L. (2016). Brexit and the law of unintended consequences. *Survival: Global Politics and Strategy*, *58*(3), 7–12.

Friedman, T. (2000). *The Lexus and the Olive Tree: Understanding globalization*. London: HarperCollins.

Gamble, A. (1994). *The free economy and the strong state: The politics of Thatcherism* (2nd ed.). Basingstoke: Macmillan.

Gamble, A. (2009). *The spectre at the feast: Capitalist crisis and the politics of recession*. Basingstoke: Palgrave.

Garrett, G. (1998). *Partisan politics in the global economy*. Cambridge: Cambridge University Press.

Geddes, A. (2013). *Britain and the European Union*. Basingstoke: Palgrave Macmillan.

Geddes, A. (2014). The EU, UKIP and the politics of immigration in Britain. *The Political Quarterly*, *85*(3), 289–295.

Giddens, A. (1990). *The consequences of modernity*. Cambridge: Polity.

Giddens, A. (1994). *Beyond left and right: The future of radical politics*. Cambridge: Polity.

Giddens, A. (1998). *The Third Way: The renewal of social democracy*. Cambridge: Polity.

Giddens, A. (2006). *Europe in the global age*. Cambridge: Polity.

Gietel-Basten, S. (2016). Why Brexit? The toxic mix of immigration and austerity. *Population and Development Review*, *42*(4), 673–680.

Gifford, C. (2006). The rise of post-imperial populism: The case of right-wing Euroscepticism in Britain. *European Journal of Political Research*, *45*, 851–869.

Gifford, C. (2014). The people against Europe: The Eurosceptic challenge to the United Kingdom's coalition government. *Journal of Common Market Studies*, *52*(3), 512–528.

Gifford, C. (2016). The United Kingdom's Eurosceptic political economy. *British Journal of Politics and International Relations*, *18*(4), 779–794.

Gill, S. (1998). European governance and new constitutionalism: Economic and monetary union and alternatives to disciplinary neo-liberalism in Europe. *New Political Economy*, *3*(1), 5–26.

Glyn, A., & Wood, S. (2001). Economic policy under New Labour: How social democratic is the Blair government? *The Political Quarterly*, *72*(1), 50–66.

Goodwin, M., & Heath, O. (2016). The 2016 referendum, Brexit and the left behind: An aggregate-level analysis of the result. *The Political Quarterly*, *87*(3), 323–332.

Gough, J. (2017). Brexit, xenophobia and left strategy now. *Capital and Class*, *41*(2), 366–372.

Greven, T. (2016). *The rise of right-wing populism in Europe and the United States: A comparative perspective*. Berlin: Friedrich-Ebert-Stiftung.

Guldi, J. (2017). The case for utopia: History and the possible meanings of Brexit a hundred years on. *Globalizations*, *14*(1), 150–156.

Gullestad, M. (2006). 'Imagined kinship: The role of descent in the rearticulation of Norwegian ethno-nationalism'. In A. Gingrich & M. Banks (Eds.), *Neo-Nationalism in Europe and beyond: Perspectives from social anthropology* (pp. 69–91). New York, NY: Berghahn Books.

Gumbrell-McCormick, R., & Hyman, R. (2017). What about the workers? The implications of Brexit for British and European labour. *Competition and Change*, *21*(3), 169–184.

Hall, P. A., & Soskice, D. (2001). *Varieties of capitalism: The institutional foundations of comparative advantage*. Oxford: Oxford University Press.

Hall, S. (1983). 'The great moving right show'. In S. Hall & M. Jacques (Eds.), *The politics of Thatcherism* (pp. 19–39). London: Lawrence and Wishart.

Hall, S. (1992). The question of cultural identity. In S. Hall, D. Held, & T. McGrew (Eds.), *Modernity and its futures* (pp. 273–325). Cambridge: Polity Press.

Hanley, L. (2017). What do we mean when we say "white working-class". *The Guardian*, March 23.

Hardy, J., & McCann, L. (2017). Brexit one year on: Introducing the Special Issue. *Competition and Change*, *21*(3), 165–168.

Harris, J. (2016). Britain is in the midst of a working-class revolt. *The Guardian*, June 17.

Harris, J. (2017). Revolutions are for zealots and fools – As the Tory Bolsheviks will find out. *The Guardian*, July 21.

Harris, R., & Charlton, M. (2016). Voting out of the European Union: Exploring the geography of Leave. *Environment and Planning A*, *48*(11), 2116–2128.

Harvey, D. (1989). *The condition of post-modernity: An enquiry into the origins of cultural change*. Oxford: Blackwell.

Hay, C. (1996). *Re-stating social and political change*. Buckingham: Open University Press.

Hay, C. (2004). Common trajectories, variable paces, divergent outcomes? Models of European capitalism under conditions of complex economic interdependence. *Review of International Political Economy*, *11*(2), 231–262.

Haylett, C. (2000). Modernization, welfare and "third way" politics: Limits to theorizing in thirds. *Transactions of the Institute of British Geographers*, *26*(1), 43–56.

Henderson, A., Jeffery, C., Liñeira, R., Scully, R., Wincott, D., & Jones, W. (2016). England, Englishness and Brexit. *The Political Quarterly*, *87*(2), 187–199.

Henley, J. (2017). 'It will be hard to go. A bit of me is dying'. The EU nationals fleeing from Britain. *The Guardian*, July 29.

Hennig, B. D., & Dorling, D. (2016). The EU referendum. *Political Insight*, *7*(2), 20–21.

Hirst, P., & Thompson, G. (2000). *Globalization in question: The international economy and the possibilities of governance* (2nd ed.). Cambridge: Polity.

Hobolt, S. B. (2009). *Europe in question: Referendums on European integration*. Oxford: Oxford University Press.

Hobolt, S. B. (2016). The Brexit vote: A divided nation, a divided continent. *Journal of European Public Policy*, *23*(9), 1259–1277.

Hobolt, S. B., & Tilley, J. (2016). Fleeing the centre: The rise of challenger parties in the aftermath of the Euro crisis. *West European Politics*, *39*(5), 971–991.

Holden, R. (1999). Labour's transformation: Searching for the point of origin – The European dynamic. *Politics*, *19*(2), 103–108.

Hooghe, L., & Marks, G. (2007). Sources of Euroscepticism. *Acta Politica*, 42(2–3), 119–127.

Höpner, M. (2007). *Coordination and organization: The two dimensions of neo-liberal capitalism*. MPIfG Discussion Paper 07/12, Cologne: Max Planck Institute for the Study of Societies.

Hutton, W. (2017). Brexit is our generation's Dunkirk, but this time there will be no salvation. *The Observer*, July 16.

Inglehart, R. F., & Norris, P. (2016). *Trump, Brexit and the rise of populism: Economic have-nots and cultural backlash*. Harvard Kennedy School Faculty Research Working Paper Series, RWP 16-026. Retrieved from https://research.hks.harvard.edu/publications/getFile.aspx?Id=1401. Accessed on March 23, 2017.

IRR. (2016). *Post-Brexit racism*. Institute of Race Relations. Retrieved from http://www.irr.org.uk/news/post-brexit-racism/. Accessed on July 23, 2017.

Jessop, B. (2017). The organic crisis of the British state: Putting Brexit in its place. *Globalizations*, 14(1), 133–141.

Jessop, B., Bonnett, K., Bromley, S., & Ling, T. (1988). *Thatcherism: A tale of two nations*. Cambridge: Polity.

Johnson, R., & Steinberg, D. L. (2004). Distinctiveness and difference within New Labour. In D. L. Steinberg & R. Johnson (Eds.), *Blairism and the war of persuasion: Labour's passive revolution* (pp. 7–22). London: Lawrence and Wishart.

Jones, E. (2016). Brexit's lessons for democracy. *Survival: Global Politics and Strategy*, 58(3), 41–49.

Jones, O. (2016). *Chavs: The demonization of the working class*. London: Verso.

Kaiser, W. (1993). To join or not to join: The "Appeasement" policy of Britain's first EEC application. In B. Brivati & H. Jones (Eds.), *From reconstruction to integration: Britain and Europe since 1945* (pp. 144–156). Leicester: Leicester University Press.

Kaufmann, E. (2014). The politics of immigration: UKIP and beyond. *The Political Quarterly*, *85*(3), 247–250.

Kaufmann, E. (2016). It's NOT the economy stupid: Brexit as a story of personal values. *British politics and policy at the LSE*. Retrieved from http://eprints.lse.ac.uk/71585/1/blogs. lse.ac.uk-Its%20NOT%20the%20economy%20stupid% 20Brexit%20as%20a%20story%20of%20personal% 20values.pdf. Accessed on July 13, 2017.

Kenny, M. (2016). The genesis of English nationalism. *Political Insight*, *7*(2), 8–11.

Kenny, M., & Pearce, N. (2016). After Brexit: The Eurosceptic dream of an Anglosphere. *Juncture*, *22*(4), 304–307.

Khaleeli, H. (2016). A frenzy of hatred: How to understand Brexit racism. *The Guardian*, June 29.

Khan, O., & Weekes-Bernard, D. (2016). *This is still about us: Why ethnic minorities see immigration differently*. London: Runnymede Trust.

Kibasi, T. (2016). Understanding Brexit: Why does it feel like this and where do we go from here? *Juncture*, *23*(1), 12–17.

Kirkland, C. (2015). Thatcherism and the origins of the 2007 crisis. *British Politics*, *10*(4), 514–535.

Kriesi, H., Grande, E., Dolezal, M., Helbling, M., Hoglinger, D., Hutter, S., & Wuest, B. (2012). *Political conflict in Western Europe*. Cambridge: Cambridge University Press.

Krippner, G. (2012). *Capitalizing on crisis: The political origins of the rise of finance*. Cambridge, MA: Harvard University Press.

Kundnani, H. (2017). Europe may seem to have its mojo back, but old problems still haunt the continent. *The Observer*, July 9.

Kynaston, D. (2002). *City of London, volume 4: A club no more 1945–2000*. London: Pimlico.

Ladrech, R. (1994). Europeanization of domestic politics and institutions: The case of France. *Journal of Common Market Studies*, 32(1), 69–98.

Lakner, C., & Milanovic, B. (2013). Global income distribution: From the fall of the Berlin Wall to the Great Recession. *The World Bank Economic Review*, 1–30.

Lanchester, J. (2016). Brexit blues. *London Review of Books*, 38(15), 3–6.

Lash, S., & Urry, J. (1987). *The end of organized capitalism*. Cambridge: Polity.

Lavery, S. (2017). The legitimation of post-crisis capitalism in the United Kingdom: Real wage decline, finance-led growth and the state. *New Political Economy*. doi:10.1080/13563467.2017.1321627.

Lee, S. (2009). The rock of stability: The political economy of the Brown government. *Policy Studies*, 30(1), 17–31.

Lipietz, A. (1987). *Mirages and miracles: The crisis of global Fordism*. London: Verso.

Lord Ashcroft Polls (2016). How the United Kingdom voted on Thursday…. And why. *Lord Ashcroft Polls*. Retrieved from http://lordashcroftpolls.com/2016/06/how-the-united-kingdom-voted-and-why/. Accessed on July 16, 2017.

Ludlow, N. P. (1997). *Dealing with Britain: The six and the first UK application to the EEC*. Cambridge: Cambridge University Press.

Lynch, P. (2012). European policy. In T. Heppel & S. Seawright (Eds.), *Cameron and the Conservatives: The transition to coalition government* (pp. 74–88). Basingstoke: Palgrave.

Lyons, K. (2016). Racist incidents feared to be linked to Brexit result. *The Guardian*, June 26.

Macshane, D. (2015). *Brexit: How Britain left Europe*. London: I.B. Tauris.

Mair, P. (2000). Partyless democracy: Solving the paradox of New Labour. *New Left Review*, 2, 21–45.

Mair, P. (2013). *Ruling the void: The hollowing of Western democracy*. London: Verso.

Mann, R., & Fenton, S. (2009). The personal contexts of national sentiments. *Journal of Ethnic and Migration Studies*, 35(4), 517–534.

Marquand, D. (2017). The people is sublime. *New Statesman*, July 21–27.

Martell, L. (2007). The third wave in globalization theory. *International Studies Review*, 9(2), 173–196.

Mason, P. (2016). Brexit is a fake revolt – Working-class culture is being hijacked to help the elite. *The Guardian*, June 20.

McKenzie, L. (2016). Brexit: A two-fingered salute from the working class. *Red Pepper*, August/September. Retrieved from http://www.redpepper.org.uk/brexit-a-two-fingered-salute-from-the-working-class/. Accessed on May 16, 2017.

McKenzie, L. (2017). "It's not ideal": Reconsidering "anger" and "apathy" in the Brexit vote among an invisible working class. *Competition and Change, 21*(3), 199–210.

Menon, A., & Salter, J.-P. (2016). Brexit: Initial reflections. *International Affairs, 92*(6), 1297–1318.

Milward, A. (2000). *The European rescue of the nation state* (2nd ed.). London: Routledge.

Morgan, J. (2017). Brexit: Be careful what you wish for. *Globalizations, 14*(1), 118–126.

Mudde, C. (2004). The populist zeitgeist. *Government and Opposition, 39*(4), 42–563.

Mudde, C. (2009). *Populist radical right parties in Europe.* Cambridge: Cambridge University Press.

Muehlebach, A., & Shoshan, N. (2012). Post-Fordist affect: Introduction. *Anthropological Quarterly, 85*(2), 317–343.

Müller, J.-W. (2016). *What is populism?* Philadelphia, PA: University of Pennsylvania Press.

NatCen Social Research. (2017). *British social attitudes survey, 2015 [data collection].* 3rd ed. UK Data Service. SN: 8116, doi:10.5255/UKDA-SN-8116-3

Nairn, T. (1973). *The left against Europe.* Harmondsworth: Penguin.

Nairn, T. (2001). Mario and the magician. *New Left Review, 9,* 5–30.

Nairn, T. (2005). Ukania: The rise of the "Annual Report" society. In T. Nairn & P. James (Eds.), *Global matrix: Nationalism, globalism and state-terrorism* (pp. 125–142). London: Pluto Press.

Needham, D. (2014). *UK monetary policy from devaluation to Thatcher 1967-82.* Basingstoke: Palgrave Macmillan.

Newman, M. (1983). *Socialism and European unity: The dilemma of the left in Britain and France.* London: Junction Books.

Nölke, A. (2017). Brexit: Towards a new global phase of organized capitalism? *Competition and Change, 21*(3), 230–241.

Nougayrède, N. (2017). As Britain bows out, Europe's moment may be at hand. *The Guardian*, June 19.

Ohmae, K. (1995). *The end of the nation state: The rise of regional economics.* London: HarperCollins.

Oliver, T. (2015). Europe's British question: The UK–EU relationship in a changing Europe and multipolar world. *Global Society, 29*(3), 409–426.

ONS. (2015). *UK labour market – September 2015.* London: ONS.

ONS. (2017). *Statistical bulletin: Migration statistics quarterly report: May 2017.* Retrieved from https://www.ons. gov.uk/peoplepopulationandcommunity/ populationandmigration/internationalmigration/bulletins/ migrationstatisticsquarterlyreport/may2017. Accessed on July 10, 2017.

O'Reilly, J., Fround, J., Johal, S., Williams, K., Warhurst, C., Morgan, G., ... Le Galès, P. (2016). Brexit: Understanding the socio-economic origins and consequences. *Socio-Economic Review*, *14*(4), 807–854.

Owen, E. (2010). Reactive, defensive and weak. In T. Finch & D. Goodhart (Eds.), *Immigration under Labour* (pp. 15–16). London: IPPR.

Pabst, A. (2016). Brexit, post-liberalism, and the politics of paradox. *Telos*, *176*, 189–201.

Panitch (2000). The new imperial state. *New Left Review*, *2*(2), 5–22.

Parker, O. (2008). Challenging "new constitutionalism" in the EU: French resistance, "social Europe" and "soft governance". *New Political Economy*, *13*(4), 397–417.

Parker, S. (Ed.). (2013). *The squeezed middle: The pressure on ordinary workers in America and Britain*. Bristol: Policy Press.

Parveen, N. (2016). Why do some ethnic minority voters want to leave the EU? *The Guardian*, June 1.

Pettifor, A. (2017). Brexit and its consequences. *Globalizations*, *14*(1), 127–132.

Polanyi, K. (1944, 2001). *The great transformation*. Boston, MA: Beacon Press.

Ray, L. (2007). *Globalization and everyday life*. London: Routledge.

Rayner, J. (2017). Jay Rayner's manifesto to keep the country fed: Brexit will affect every aspect of our food chain and imperils the health of the nation. *The Observer*, July 30.

Reay, D. (2007). A darker shade of pale? Whiteness, the middle-classes and multi-ethnic inner city schooling. *Sociology*, *41*(6), 1041–1060.

Rhodes, J. (2009). The political breakthrough of the BNP: The case of Burnley. *British Politics*, *4*(1), 22–46.

Rhodes, J. (2011). It's not just them. It's whites as well: Whiteness, class and BNP support. *Sociology*, *45*(1), 102–117.

Runciman, D. (2016). A win for proper people? Brexit as a rejection of the networked world. *Juncturem*, *23*(1), 4–7.

Runciman, W. (1966). *Relative deprivation and social justice*. Berkeley, CA: University of California Press.

Savage, M., Cunningham, N., & Divine, F. (2015). *Social class in the 21st century*. London: Penguin.

Seaton, J. (2016). Brexit and the media. *The Political Quarterly*, *87*(3), 333–337.

Seymour, R. (2015). UKIP and the crisis of Britain. In L. Panitch & G. Albo (Eds.), *Socialist register 2016: The politics of the right* (pp. 24–50). London: Merlin Press.

Simon, R. (1982). *Gramsci's political thought: An introduction*. London: Lawrence and Wishart.

Skeggs, B. (2000). *Formations of class and gender*. London: Sage.

Skeggs, B. (2004). *Class, self and culture*. London: Routledge.

Soros, G. (1998). *The crisis of global capitalism: Open society endangered*. New York, NY: Public Affairs.

Spencer, S. (2010). Economic gain, political cost. In T. Finch & D. Goodhart (Eds.), *Immigration under Labour* (pp. 19–20). London: IPPR.

Steinberg, D. L., & Johnson, R. (2004). Blairism and the war of persuasion: Labour's passive revolution. In D. L. Steinberg &

R. Johnson (Eds.), *Blairism and the war of persuasion: Labour's passive revolution* (pp. 23–37). London: Lawrence and Wishart.

Strange, G. (2006). The left against Europe? A critical engagement with new constitutionalism and structural dependency theory. *Government and Opposition*, 41(2), 197–229.

Strathern, M. (1995). Nostalgia and the new genetics. In D. Battaglia (Ed.), *Rhetorics of self-making* (pp. 97–120). Berkeley, CA: University of California Press.

Streeck, W. (2014). *Buying time: The delayed crisis of democratic capitalism*. London: Verso.

Streeck, W. (2015). *The rise of the European consolidation state*. MPIfG Discussion Paper 15/1. Max Planck Institute for the Study of Societies, Cologne.

Swales, K. (2016). *Understanding the Leave vote*. London: NatCen Social Research.

Taggart, P. (1998). A touchstone of dissent: Euroscepticism in contemporary Western European party systems. *European Journal of Political Research*, *33*, 363–388.

Taggart, P. (2000). *Populism*. Buckingham: Open University Press.

Thorleifsson, C. (2016). From coal to UKIP: The struggle over identity in post-industrial Doncaster. *History and Anthropology*, *27*(5), 555–568.

Tombs, R. (2016). Brexit, the English revolt: Euroscepticism and the future of the United Kingdom. *New Statesman*, July 16.

Tombs, R. (2017). The age of volatility. *New Statesman*, July 14–20.

Tomlinson, S., & Dorling, D. (2016). Brexit has its roots in the British Empire – so how do we explain it to the young. *New Statesman*, May 9.

Tournier-Sol, K. (2015). Reworking the Eurosceptic and conservative traditions into a populist narrative: UKIP's Winning Formula? *Journal of Common Market Studies*, 53(1), 140–156.

Travis, A. (2017). EU nationals must join register to stay under May's plans. *The Guardian*, June 27.

TUC. (2015). *In parts of Britain half of jobs pay less than the living wage*. Retrieved from https://www.tuc.org.uk/economic-issues/labour-market-and-economic-reports/britain-needs-pay-rise/fair-pay-fortnight-2015. Accessed on July 9, 2017.

TUC. (2016a). *Working people must not pay the price for the vote to Leave*. London: TUC.

TUC. (2016b). *UK employment rights and the EU: Assessment of the impact of membership of the European Union on employment rights in the UK*. London: TUC.

TUC. (2016c). *UK workers experienced sharpest wage fall of any leading economy*. Retrieved from https://www.tuc.org.uk/economic-issues/labour-market/uk-workers-experienced-sharpest-wage-fall-any-leading-economy-tuc. Accessed on July 09, 2017.

Tuck, R. (2016). The left case for Brexit. *Dissent*, June 6. Retrieved from https://www.dissentmagazine.org/online_articles/left-case-brexit. Accessed on July 05, 2017.

Urry, J. (2003). *Global complexity*. Cambridge: Polity.

Usherwood, S., & Startin, N. (2013). Euroscepticism as a persistent phenomenon. *Journal of Common Market Studies*, *51*(1), 1–16.

Vail, M. I. (2014). Between One-Nation Toryism and neo-liberalism: The dilemmas of British Conservatism and Britain's evolving place in Europe. *Journal of Common Market Studies*, *53*(1), 106–122.

Van Apeldoorn, B. (2001). 'The struggle over European order: Transnational class agency in the making of "embedded neo-liberalism"'. In A. Bieler & A. D. Morton (Eds.), *Social forces in the making of the new Europe: The restructuring of European social relations in the global political economy* (pp. 70–92). Basingstoke: Palgrave.

Van Apeldoorn, B. (2002). *Transnational capitalism and the struggle over European integration*. London: Routledge.

Vasilopoulou, S. (2013). Continuity and change in the study of Euroscepticism: Plus ça change. *Journal of Common Market Studies*, *51*(1), 153–168.

Versi, M. (2016). Brexit has given voice to racism – and too many are complicit. *The Guardian*, June 27.

Vote Leave (2016). *The European Union and your family: The facts*. London: Vote Leave.

Walker, P. (2016). Nigel Farage basks in the triumph of his new dawn. *The Guardian*, June 24.

Walker, P. (2017). Corbyn picked up support of anti-Brexiters in election. *The Guardian*, August 2.

Walker, I., & Smith, H. J. (2002). Fifty years of relative deprivation research. In I. Walker & H. J. Smith (Eds.), *Relative deprivation: Specification, development and integration* (pp. 1–12). Cambridge: Cambridge University Press.

Walker, I., Wong, N., & Kretzschmar, K. (2002). Relative deprivation and attribution: From grievance to action. In I. Walker & H. J. Smith (Eds.), *Relative deprivation: Specification, development and integration* (pp. 288–312). Cambridge: Cambridge University Press.

Wallace, W. (1991). Pride and prejudice. *Marxism Today*, (October), 28–31.

Watkins, S. (2016). Casting off? *New Left Review*, *100*, 5–31.

Watt, N., & Wintour, P. (2015). How immigration came to haunt Labour: The inside story. *The Guardian*, March 24.

Wellings, B. (2002). Empire-Nation: National and imperial discourses in English nationalism. *Nations and Nationalism*, *8*(1), 95–109.

Wellings, B. (2010). Losing the peace: Euroscepticism and the foundations of contemporary English nationalism. *Nations and Nationalism*, *16*(3), 488–505.

Wellings, B. (2012). *Euroscepticism and English nationalism: Losing the peace*. Bern: Peter Lang.

Wellings, B., & Baxendale, H. (2015). Euroscepticism and the Anglosphere: Traditions and dilemmas in contemporary English nationalism. *Journal of Common Market Studies*, *53*(1), 123–139.

Winlow, S., Hall, S., & Treadwell, J. (2017). *The rise of the right: English nationalism and the transformation of working class politics*. Bristol: Policy Press.

Woolas, P. (2010). Untying the gag. In T. Finch &
D. Goodhart (Eds.), *Immigration under Labour* (pp. 34–35).
London: IPPR.

Worth, O. (2017). Reviving Hayek's dream. *Globalizations*,
14(1), 104–109.

Wyn Jones, R., Henderson, A., & Wincott, D. (2012). *The
dog that finally barked: England as an emerging political
community*. London: IPPR.

Wyn Jones, R., Jeffery, C., Gottfried, G., Scully, R.,
Henderson, A., & Wincott, D. (2013). *England and its two
unions: The anatomy of a nation and its discontents*.
London: IPPR.

YouGov (2016). *How Britain voted*. Retrieved from https://
yougov.co.uk/news/2016/06/27/how-britain-voted/. Accessed
on July 9, 2017.

Younge, G. (2016). Brexit: A disaster decades in the making.
The Guardian, June 30. Retrieved from https://www.
theguardian.com/politics/2016/jun/30/brexit-disaster-decades-
in-the-making. Accessed on March 26, 2017.

Zakaria, F. (2003). *The future of freedom: Illiberal
democracy at home and abroad*. New York, NY: W.W.
Norton.

INDEX